AF784532

Representation Versus Direct Democracy in Fighting About Taxes

Representation Versus Direct Democracy in Fighting About Taxes

Conflicting Notions of Sovereignty, Legitimacy, and Civility in Relation to a Tax Fight, Watertown, Massachusetts, 1953-59

Lewis A. Dexter

Schenkman Publishing Company Inc.
Cambridge, Massachusetts

Schenkman Publishing Company Inc.
3 Mount Auburn Place
Cambridge, Massachusetts 02138

Library of Congress Cataloging in Publication Data
Dexter, Lewis Anthony.
Representation versus direct democracy in fighting about taxes.
Includes bibliographical references.
1. Watertown (Mass.)–Political and government. 2. Taxation–Massachusetts–Watertown. 3. Local government–United States–Case studies. 4. Representative government and representation–United States–Case studies. I. Title.
JS1536.W3D49 320.8′0973 81-9421
ISBN 0-87073-425-3 AACR2
ISBN 0-87073-426-1 (pbk.)

Printed in the United States of America

Contents

Introduction

Margaret Mead was best known for her early work on coming of age in Samoa and later in Papua New Guinea. But she also wove a seamless web of interest in human universals. She avoided arbitrary distinctions between people with writing and those without. Whether pre-literate or TV-addicted contemporaries, the people she studied revealed important techniques and social processes for organizing themselves into concentric circles of communities, as readers will remember from *New Lives for Old.* She was fascinated, as I am, in how leaders and followers in such networks interact to provide both continuity and change.

Lewis Dexter, author of this fine-grained case study of the citizenry of Watertown, Massachusetts, in mid-20th century, was first brought to my attention by Dr. Mead in 1954, a few years before he was starting field work in Watertown. She neglected to tell me that Prof. Dexter is linked by blood and history to Susan B. Anthony. Instead, she focused on the reasons why I should get to know Dexter's work: anthropologists ought to work everywhere they find people. Some of the best "anthropology" she said she knew was being done in Washington by Lewis Dexter, who was actually finding out about making legislation in the Congress by watching what legislators do, not merely what they say.

Mead was joined in her interest in Dexter's inquiries by Dr. Eliot D. Chapple, who, with Mead, was then hiring me as director of the Society for Applied Anthropology's Clearinghouse for Research in Human Organization. Chapple, who had helped introduce Dexter to anthropology at Harvard, was no stranger to studies of American communities, having worked on the structures and manners and customs of Newburyport, Massachusetts, through W. Lloyd Warner's Yankee City series. Harvard in the early 1930's also brought Chapple into contact with Conrad M. Arensberg, Solon T. Kimball, and F. L. W. Richardson, all to become founders, in 1941, of the Society for Applied Anthropology. They became anthropological "brothers" to Lewis Dexter, whose insights, perceptions, and some of his research methods have been influenced by these leaders in the study of human interaction. These approaches are described, in part, in Chapple and Coon's *Principles of Anthropology* (1941 and 1978) and Arensberg and Kimball's *Culture and Community* (1965).

Prof. Dexter's work stands on its own without reference to the influences of anthropologists on him or what anthropologists can learn from his participant-observation approach, supplemented by reliance on history and cross-cultural contrasts and comparisons. Alfred Schenkman Publishers deserve applause for bringing to a wider public this research, with its commentaries from the human sciences that is personal, reflecting on the life experience of its author. Objectivity rests on accurate reporting of sequences of verifiable events and not in the denial of the uniqueness of the role or personality of the observer. Dexter is a gifted teacher, and that is reflected in his being sure that the reader is never allowed to separate theory (e.g., Edmund Burke, David B. Truman, E. E. Schattschneider, and Mark Swartz) from the practice of politics by politicians and voters. We also learn from Dexter's life experience that the ethos of neighboring Belmont is different from Watertown, the "mother of the West," with its propertied *and* landless citizens combining to fight the first signs of inflation growing out of the Korean war but fighting each other over scarce resources.

As a Southerner who mistakenly thought that all Northerners were "Yankees," I relish Dexter's accounts of how waves and layers of immigration—old Yankee, the Irish, and the Armenians—produced a trade-off of myths and symbols about those ancient human concepts of sovereignty, liberty, responsibility, autonomy, and civility. A psychiatrist friend of mine, much addicted to Zorba the Greek as a metaphor of Christianity and the human condition, says of Zorba, "It's all there." Marcel

Mauss also tells us that "in the concrete is the whole." The same could be said of Dexter's microcosmic report on Watertown at that "point in time" of nearly a decade in the 1950's. He tells us of social amnesia, the role of kinship, the resentment against newcomers, the ambivalence between the insiders and outsiders (as noted also by Robert K. Merton). He stresses the place of gender, age, property, and ethnicity in shaping one's time perspective and world view vis-a-vis the politics of collecting taxes and managing the public purse. Moreover, he provides readers of Edward Shils' *Center and Periphery* (1975) and Robert Redfield's *The Little Community* (1955) with a larger study of the links between a small community and a complex, incipient "welfare state" whose political, administrative, and intellectual agents reduce the control of "the natives" over their own local affairs. And Dexter generously refers to J. P. Marquand, the novelist, for further insight into a phenomenon he also came upon: children of earlier town leaders going away and becoming part of a larger regional or national professional and business group, leaving leadership to the newcomers. Professional managers began to dilute the blood of family-owned enterprises, with the corresponding shift in the role of business as a system of power. Dexter's friend, David Riesman, would join me in delighting over some of the dramatic faces in the Watertown crowd of then 40,000 souls. Though not a novelist, Dexter whets my curiosity about the fates and threads of American history which bring together Citizen Robinson, Old American, with Citizen Hagopian, a living link with the vivid memories of a holocaust in Turkey and other Armenian massacres which undergird the motives of new Americans to participate in "pure" town meeting democracy rather than merely ratifying others' decisions. (Dexter's insights on the politics of perception reveal a lot about how controversy, while "fun" for some, might have been avoided by a tighter definition of a town meeting.)

For readers of this case study who want to leap into the action right away and come back to the hypotheses and historical-philosophical interpretations later, I suggest that you start with the chronology of events in the tax-wages fight. That is the hard core. Dexter's reconstruction of these micro-episodes gives us a clue to decision-making at "the local level." The fuss which grew out of fuzziness about defining a town meeting also reflects the spectrum of views around the proposition, with shades of John Locke, that property makes some citizens more equal than others. The chronology reminds me of Erik Erikson's step-by-step account of the Ahmadebad textile strike in *Gandhi's Truth.*

Reflecting on the Watertown base line of the 1950's, one can hope that similar studies are now under way in various other American communities to better understand the drama of local government in the 1980's as the Reagan administration attempts its radical reversals of the role of the federal establishment. That is an assignment big enough for a whole army of political scientists, anthropologists, psychiatrists, economists, and, yes, playwrights and novelists.

Wilton S. Dillon
Smithsonian Institution

1

What This Report Is About[1]

This report shows how a political unit was: first, restructured in response to population growth and ethnic competition. And then, how, after restructuring, it was exposed to much tension and risk as a result of a fight about tax rates arising out of:

(1) further changes in the in-migrant population
(2) post-Korean-War inflation
(3) alterations over time in the career and status evaluation of government employment and
(4) above all the fuzziness and, probably deliberate, equivocation of the redefining statute.

But these matters would not justify the author in asking for general attention to the report. *It is, however, of general importance.* This is because the situation demonstrates in a cogent way some basic, recurring, and inadequately illustrated patterns and problems of politics.

The Most Significant Value of This Report

The report throws light, in particular, on one very fundamental political pattern and process. That is this: a set of values, doctrines, and beliefs, become venerated and are regarded as basic truths about the political system. However, in practice, serious political people qualify these doctrines by (1) a set of practical operating rules and (2) by a conscious or unconscious awareness of offseting, counterbalancing doctrines and values.

But, from time to time, there enter into the situation a set of believers in the complete truth of some basic doctrine—or at least people who think they believe in it absolutely appear. They may be naive; they may in fact have particular interests of their own which fit or can be fitted particularly neatly into the traditional doctrine. In Watertown, in the instant circumstances, practical interests stimulated concern with and reaffirmation of naively held doctrines. In any case, such believers try to be sincere—and in so doing upset or threaten to upset the subtle sophistications of practical political life.

In Anglo-American history, the English Civil War of the 1640s involved a number of such true believers on both sides. King Charles I[2], unlike his two immediate predecessors, Elizabeth the Great and James I and VI, literally believed that, here and now, kings should exercise their divine right to govern in the full sense of the term. Elizabeth, to be sure, used some pretty tough language about her prerogative at times; James wrote a political treatise on the divine right of kings. But, when pressures and practicalities pushed them, both of them could and did climb down from their high horses; Charles found such a surrender of principle tougher to make. And, on the other side, the Parliamentary opposition included a good many zealots who reached back to other texts in the Bible or other traditions of English history and insisted that all must always live by these as they interpreted them.

Similarly, in their more rhetorical moments, the most articulate protagonists of both sides in the American Revolution exemplified the same zeal at living by doctrine and myth. On the one hand, the Americans had a profound and up to a point literal belief in the rights of free men—a belief which is now widely accepted as the American creed about freedom, human rights, and so on. On the other, the British cabinet and court (notably including that highly principled man, George III) maintained stalwart and unyielding support for the principle of parliamentary onmicompetence—and a willingness to sacrifice an empire for that principle. It is worth noting that Edmund Burke's famous speech[3] on conciliation with the colonies does not attack that principle head on. Rather, in a characteristically Burkean fashion, it pleads that government sacrifice the principled insistence on pushing a doctrine to extremes and try to act with common sense and human considerateness.

But to study the interplay of principle, interest, doctrine, value, and myth in the grand battles of 1639–1659 or 1763–1783 demands an enormous mastery of an infinity of details and relationships. Only a person who chooses to make the history of a period a major avocation has a hope of obtaining such a mastery. There are so many shades of principle. There are so many competing factions and interests. There is such a multitude of shifts of alignment. So, it becomes necessary, in order to master such periods, to oversimplify historical complexity to see them as whole.

This is not, of course, an argument against studying such portentous civil commotions as the English Civil War and the American Revolution. But it is to suggest that there is a need and a place for reports on more localized conflicts over principle—conflicts which never in fact resulted in the breakdown of government and the resort to violence. The battle in Watertown, Massachusetts, 1953–59, over town salaries and wages and tax rates was precisely such a conflict; one which, in itself, would be little noted nor long remembered outside the boundries of Watertown, itself, but nevertheless involving all the complex interplay of interest and principle. The case is of more value than most local cases because it happened to focus on the very meaning of "town meeting"—town meetings having been celebrated for a century and a half as the archpattern of popular government—and did indeed result in a fundamental battle over, in a sense, sovereignty. It brought to awareness, too, enduring questions about fair representation, about the morality of tax-wage decisions in the public arena, and of the impact of sociological factors on long established institutions.

Other Important Aspects of The Report

The report should be valuable too, because: (1) it fits quite directly into a key point of Schattschneider's *Semi-Sovereign People.*[4] He makes much of the finding that when additional parties join into a conflict it changes not only the *scope* but the *nature* of the conflict. Here in Watertown the outsiders who joined in had an unquestioned legal claim and right to do so. But they had been for the most part, politically, nobodies, indifferent and apathetic, or they were—more of them—new migrants to town. When they joined in, they were upset by familiar stratagems, but their own techniques, vice versa, upset the "establishment." Civility and courtesy became issues. And, ultimately, some reaffirmed, others queried, notions about democracy which had long been uncritically taken for granted.

(2) The new groups who found familiar stratagems distasteful had expected to be treated benignly. They felt sure that they as citizens were acting in a constitutionally sanctioned way to right a wrong. They were startled and upset when their opponents, the insiders, employed characteristic tactics of town politics, stratagems almost mythologized themselves in sagas about fights between giants of old, Yankee and Irish, in the town meeting. On the other hand, the insiders, perhaps because they had not been effectively challenged for twenty-five years, found that the outsiders went far beyond the area of fairness. For the outsiders attacked the honesty of the intentions of the insiders. This was regarded by the latter—who often saw themselves as career workers for the town, not just as job-holders—as indecent. That sort of personal attack was not, and never had been, characteristic of town meeting politics in Watertown (or probably in similar Massachusetts towns). Indeed, it is hard to see how open town meetings could have flourished over the years unless active figures in the meeting avoided the kind of attack in which the newcomers engaged. This aspect of the situation makes the case relevant to Fred Bailey's profound work on *Stratagems and Spoils*.[5] Although Bailey, and others who may loosely be described as Machiavellian, are correct in pointing out that faction leaders constantly bend the rules to their own advantage if they can, such writers probably do not stress enough that "rules of the game," are functional.[6] They prevent the development of bitter personal resentment—as is well known to students of Congressional procedure, of course.[7] But what may not be widely enough recognized[8] is that naive men of conscience, true believers, persons convinced of their own morality, are particularly likely to threaten the rules of the game. They find it natural—sincere—to attack their opponents as indecent or wicked. Fortunately for Watertown, this tendency did not go very far there; but it went far enough to exemplify the danger of principled men of innocence in politics;

a danger which the United States saw to a greater extent in the 60s, and which Iran is seeing today.

(3) The report also shows in concrete form an aspect of "local-level politics" as defined by Swartz.[9] Major political disputes, seemingly local, may be a function of taken-for-granted administrative patterns and processes of some larger political unit. In this case, almost all the outsiders and most of the insiders looked at the fight as one about the tax rate: how much should the tax rate be raised to pay for increases in the wages of town employees? But in fact, as we shall see, the great proportion of the tax rate increase was due to increased expenditures which were required by the State of Massachusetts or its agencies. Under state law and practice, the School Committee budget may not be touched or reduced by the town. Yet, the greater part of what were seen as town wage increases were for the schools. In fiscal 1956, for instance, out of the town's total expenditures for everything of $8,534,000, $1,313.000 was for teacher salaries; and, of course, there were many increased expenditures for maintenance and equipment in the schools, additionally.

And, in addition to the school budget, the greater part of the town's increased expenditures during the years in question were due to assessments from other agencies which the town could not control. These assessments were made by the Metropolitan Transportation Agency and the Metropolitan District Commission (which runs parks, sewers, and so on) and from the County (which managed, for instance, some prisons). And, finally, the town had become heavily dependent upon the state for fundings coming from state-collected taxes; for various reasons, the state decided in one of the key years in question to allow the localities less from these taxes.

The point of all this is, of course, that the town was not in the 1950s an independent unit, run by its own town meeting, even though most people in town (and in other Massachusetts towns) thought it was. The control by other agencies was to most Watertowners obscure. But, in fact, silently, or almost so, on little cat feet, for seventy-five years, the Commonwealth of Massachusetts had taken over control of the majority of town expenditures. Much of this was a probable (though whether or not necessary can be debated) result of the growth of the welfare state in Massachusetts. something which happened earlier than in other states.

Beyond this, it may be worth following out Swartz's definition of local level politics as being "multiplex," consisting of many strands, "where politics is incomplete in the sense that actors outside the range of the local . . . relationships are vitally and directly involved in the politics of the local group."[10]

(4) In fact, the state was vitally, directly, and even decisively involved in what happened in Watertown on most matters. But political actors in Watertown did not in general perceive this. Even those who unquestionably knew it as a fact disregarded it when they took part in town conflicts. They did not bother to formulate or explain the actual situation. An honest man, like Miles Robinson, as Chairman of the Finance Committee, knew of course how gravely the state affected Watertown expenditures. But in his blast at wastefulness in town, he blithely disregarded what he unquestionably knew. One might say: well, that was to his interest in the fight over town expenditures. So, it is particularly significant to note that the people on the other side, the great majority of town officials, the Selectmen, for instance, in defending the tax rate usually failed to mention state-mandated expenditures. They, too, like Robinson, treated the issues as entirely within the competence of the town. It would take, possibly, a detailed psychobiographical study to be certain why these highly pertinent factors were not much discussed or were overlooked by those whose interest it was to stress them.

But two hypotheses, or perhaps three, suggest themselves. First, the arena of open conflict within the town was more exciting and challenging. It was, at least to the insiders, in a way fun, although in a way exasperating. Second, everybody actively engaged in the controversy had learned the established myths about town meeting autonomy and control. Challenging them—or doubting them—would have been unorthodox. And, third, the insiders at least enjoyed holding town office because it gave them a feeling of competence. To blame everything, or much, on the state, though correct, would have been to assert their own weakness.

In general terms, then, this case throws some light on a neglected area of political analysis: the politics of perception or focus. How does it happen that some objectively important aspects of a situation are not attended to while others occupy the foreground?[11]

(5) Within its limits, the case directly disproves a rather natural outgrowth of the emphasis upon compromise by many Anglo-American political scientists and politicians. A bad offender in this regard is a book by Bauer, Pool, and *Dexter.*[12] We say: "the only thing in a democracy that parliament must not do is (to) settle controversial issues." We maintained that in principle legislative decisions should be so phrased that each side can suppose that it has not entirely lost and has a chance to win on the next go-around. Now, in general terms, this may be correct—and traces back to the old Chinese proverb about letting your enemy have an opportunity to escape on a bridge of gold. But the particular implication which we seem to have drawn from it, which we intended, and which is well spoken of by political pragmatists, is that it is desirable to be equivocal and ambiguous. From a strictly short-run political standpoint, this may generally be true.

But, in the particular Watertown case, and in many others, the whole saddening, harassing, difficult, expensive fight would never have arisen if the original statute had defined "town meeting" clearly. As we shall see, although there were elements of difficulty anyhow, they would not have developed then and there except for the failure to define town meeting. Perhaps—I was unable to ascertain the historical-political situation in 1919 and following years precisely—perhaps the only way to get the original act, establishing the limited town meeting, was to phrase it ambiguously, so each side could believe it had won. But, in the quiet years, the 1930s or early 1940s, it would certainly have been easy enough had anybody had enough foresight to redraft the previous statute and clarify it. And if it was not necessary in 1919 to be fuzzy and equivocal, then it was irresponsible to be so.

So, thinking about this case leads to a conclusion quite different from our statement in Bauer, Pool, and Dexter. Had I reflected on this first, I would have insisted that in Bauer, Pool, and Dexter, we should have said "It is possible in some instances—and perhaps the Reciprocal Trade Extension Acts of 1953, 1954, and 1955, were such cases—that bitter, knockdown fights can be avoided by making a statute or agreement sufficiently vague so that it appears unsettled. But, nevertheless, there is always a risk in failing to settle matters."

(6) The situation in Watertown raises questions about the value of status homogeneity for political stability, or rather, the danger of status lack of homogeneity. The old Yankees, as one of the prominent figures in the situation claimed, may have acted as governors on the automobile of town politics. But, he pointed out, they had moved out, and no similar governing class had taken their place. Accordingly, there was nobody from 1953 to 1959 in town who could settle issues in the way that men, looking back, believed the old Yankees could from 1900 to 1940–and the way certain high status groups could in other, adjoining communities, such as Belmont.

Gamson has made a study of conflict in 18 New England communities, comparing nine where conflict was rancorous with nine where it was less so.[13] He reports that rancor was more apt to develop where there was structural strain–a new group of people trying to "take over" from the older ones; the Homeowners against the Irish, might well be a source of such structural strain. He reports also that rancor is more apt to develop where there is a lack of friendship on the personal level between members of different factions; the Homeowners being outsiders probably had fewer such relationships with the town leaders and employees in the 1950s than the latter had, when, as a minority, they had opposed the old Yankees. So, the present town leaders looked back to the relationship between them and the Yankees as a model for what ought to be between the Homeowners and them? Gamson goes ahead and states also that a lack of organizational ties and interpersonal ties between members of different factions correlated with an increased degree of rancor; such a lack was evidently present in Watertown in the situation under discussion.

2

The Structure of Watertown's Town Meeting

Watertown was run, like about forty other Massachusetts communities, during the period in question,[14] by a limited town meeting. This type of local government was found, for all practical purposes, only in Massachusetts, Connecticut, and Brattleboro, Vermont. It is an outgrowth, of course, of the true town meeting, under which most municipalities in New England were governed. In a true town meeting, in theory, everybody has a right to take part and to vote on all the numerous town positions, right down to dog-catcher and tree-warden, and on all the articles–in modern times, at least, often complex–in the warrant (agenda). Now, in fact, the reason the true town meeting works is that most of the time most people exercise the right only superficially. In fact, there have been occasions when town meetings could not get a quorum and had to send out police to pull voters in. Nevertheless, during the nineteenth century, and to some extent the eighteenth–under the leadership of men like Samuel Adams, Elbridge Gerry, Joseph Hawley, and, more indirectly, Jefferson and Jackson and their heirs–the notion grew up that the people really did control the town meeting. Massachusetts orators lauded rhetorically the way in which New England alone in the world (except for a few Swiss cantons) let the people rule–although a very little observation would have sufficed to show that Massachusetts towns were generally in fact run by the few who bothered and had the capacity and leisure to master the complexities of governance. In fact, until after 1850, the Massachusetts courts did not accept this notion of democratic town control. What the town meeting did do, at times and places, was give the public a clear opportunity to say "Yes" or "No" on a wider variety of issues than did other forms of local government.

But after 1890 many of the towns, especially towns suburban to Boston and Springfield, grew larger. Thousands of people became eligible to vote. The sheer mechanics of a town meeting thus became difficult. How could all these electors be gathered in one place and hear each other speak? Still more: what would happen if a large number of voters wanted to take part in contested roll calls, controversies, and parliamentary maneuvers? This sheer growth in numbers was accompanied, inevitably in the circumstances of immigration, by a decline in homogeneity. Where the electorate of the towns was once Yankee and Protestant, now it came to include large numbers of Catholics from different ethnic backgrounds. Where the electorate of the towns had once included some fairly prosperous farmers, now farming declined, and other occupations took its place.

However, the traditional value which had become attached to town meeting democracy—the cluster of myth which had grown up around the town meeting, the sense of towns as virtuous and cities as depraved, a feeling much accentuated by the suspicion of big, bad Boston in the rest of the state—made most towns reluctant to take the obvious step and incorporate themselves as cities. There was also a strong practical incentive for the towns to continue from a statutory standpoint as towns and not become cities: "The legislature traditionally put greater restrictions on cities"[15] than on towns, this also because at least until 1940 legislators tended to regard cities as less virtuous than towns and in greater need of control. In so feeling, of course, legislators simply shared the general presuppositions of middle-class Americans, reported for instance by C. Wright Mills, in his famous analysis of social problems texts.[16] Therefore, the legislature required that in cities policement and firemen be under civil service whereas in towns they did not have to be. But tax-conscious Finance Committees would prefer that police and fire be outside the civil service so that there would be less of a pension burden on the town over a period of years[17] – and also so that police and fire would be more reluctant to bargain aggressively for wage rises and fringe benefits.[18]

Also, right after the First World War, there was an effort in many ways for old stock American Protestants to try to bolster themselves against "foreign" groups and stocks. The Federal Immigration legislation of that period is of course a dramatic example. The revisions of the Massachusetts constitution of 1780 in the immediate postwar years were largely directed towards the same end; Massachusetts government was made very complex, to prevent any Governor from controlling it. In fact, the Governor was left with very little power of initial appointment because so many official terms became overlapping. Basically, the reason for this was fear that some one like James Michael Curley, a hero to many of the poorer Boston Irish, would become Governor. (In fact, he did, twenty years later, for one term). It should be added that many of the up-country and lace-curtain Irish were, by this time, just as suspicious of the appeal of a Curley to the city mobs as the Old Yankees were. That is to say, there was mixture of fear of foreign elements and fear of mob rule.

Obviously, the moving into the suburban towns of the "foreign" elements created apprehension. So, along with the administrative reasons for regulating and limiting the town meeting, there was this fear. Possibly, also, the dominantly male leaders of the suburban towns may, with women's suffrage and the greater amount of time spent by women in the towns, have felt that women too, constituted a threat. In fact, the limited town meeting suburban towns were still in 1950 chiefly dominated by men; a careful comparative study might show that this was not as true elsewhere in the country, but that is as of now sheer speculation.

In the event, as we shall see, the Watertown limited town meeting did not keep the Irish from control. For in the 1940s, what were left of the old Yankees largely moved out of town.

What Was a Limited, Representative Town Meeting?

Watertown was the third town to adopt a limited town meeting–Brookline in 1919 having been the first. A limited town meeting–or as it is often called a representative town meeting–

simply means that each precinct in town elects a number of members to the town meeting, so called; and that town meeting does all, or nearly all, the things which the town meeting formerly did. In Watertown, as in most towns, town meeting members served for three years, with approximately one-third being elected annually. Watertown was in the 1950s divided into ten precincts, each of which elected twenty-seven town meeting members to serve for three years. Thirty-nine elected town officials also were fully voting town meeting members. The total of 309 meant that, for the most part, a representative town meeting could be viewed as a very large town council. However, as of right, on most matters, subject of course to the other right of voting members to restrict debate, any voter in principle had the right to speak. Of course, if many voters had claimed the right with an electorate of thousands, the system would have broken down.

Since nearly all town meeting members were employed, and since the body was large, it necessarily relied upon committees and upon the executive. The executive consisted chiefly of the three Selectmen. The most powerful committee in Watertown as in most towns was the Finance Committee.

Service in the town meeting involved a moderately heavy commitment of time. Members had to expect in the period under consideration to spend twenty-four hours actually in meetings, at least. They got, in Watertown, phone calls from constituents. This was quite different from adjoining Belmont where the hall in which the limited town meeting met was not even large enough to hold all elected members if they had all chosen to come the same night. In Watertown most important town committees on average seem to have held throughout the year ten committee meetings of several hours each; the Finance Committee considerably more.

Under the theory and practice of citizen democracy, all town meeting memberships and committee memberships were unpaid (the officers were paid). A person employed in a typical kind of job would get no particular benefit from such service to the town. Since by 1950 most jobs for Watertowners were outside Watertown—in Boston, Cambridge, or Waltham, for example—employers would neither know nor care about the demands of town meeting membership. A salesman or researcher, who had to work several evenings (especially on Mondays when town meetings were usually held) would not be able to do the job justice. Indeed, since town meetings very often, committee meetings frequently, ran late, members could expect to be sleepy the following day.

Some towns—notably Belmont, mentioned above—have met the situation by turning the town meeting into a ratifying body, an agency of last resort. But Watertown did not take this route. For one thing, it has an unusually high proportion of fourth-generation Irish, who, in Massachusetts, as elsewhere, are heavily oriented towards the fun and games of politics. Unlike many adjoining towns, most town employees lived in the town. Unlike most adjoining towns by 1950, there were large groups of kin, second and third cousins, in town; as we shall see, this very fact created much resentment among political newcomers. And unlike some adjoining towns, notably Belmont, with its high proportion of famous scholars and prominent businessmen, the Watertown permanent residents were not much oriented beyond the locality; few of them were even oriented towards state politics (which I heard discussed only two or three times during the whole set of interviews; I never heard any mention of any national or cosmopolitan issue). Yet Watertowners were good citizens, steady people, and the great majority of them did work in the area (unlike, say, Framingham or Needham, with their high proportion of travelling salesmen).

But, of course, given the situation, the people who got elected to town meeting would be people who would not lose much by it, to whom it was not unrewarding. But note the underlying point: *in Watertown,* unlike many towns, such as Belmont, *town meeting members did what they are supposed to do in democratic theory.* They considered, discussed, paid attention, debated, spent time. The classic ideal of citizenship was well exemplified in them. But this meant that, of necessity, town employees and their relatives were disproportionately elected to town meeting. They could afford the time. It was not for them unrewarding; it might even be rewarding. They knew what the discussion and debate was about, up to a point. "And their relatives . . ." is true because the kind of jobs which relatives of town employees got, when not employed by the town, were likely to be with the Federal government (post office, for instance), with the public utilities, and the like—with such employers likely to let them spend time on town matters, that is.

But when the fight to be described broke out, town meeting came under bitter attack for this very reason. There was vehement debate on the question: how many votes do town meeting members control? At the lowest estimate, the number was in one sense substantial, although that depends on the definition of control. Not every man controls his brother's vote. Two statements made by the "Homeowners" in their publicity bear on the issue: they argued that "62 or more salaried town meeting members represent 700 town employees." At other times they argued "115 employees or their blood relatives, living in the same house, sit in town meeting." The precise figure could have been argued until doomsday; house, blood relative, etc., all are terms subject to controversy. Fundamentally, however, it was true: a very disproportionate number of town meeting members would be inclined to identify with town employees—although such statements as that by one of the taxpayers leaders: "I told everyone in my neighborhood that eighteen out of twenty-seven town meeting members (from our precinct) were town employees," were formally false.

The Citizens Committee, the organization of town employees and their supporters, defended them by as they put it "nailing" "the Big Lie" of the Homeowners. "The Big Lie—Employees control the town meeting. The truth: only 24 percent are employees . . ." (Which is a little more than the figure of 62 claimed by the Homeowners).

But a leader of that Citizens Committee privately made a much more profound case: "There are hundreds of (nuclear) families in Watertown which have some relative in the town meeting. There could be a possibility that some one is not related to a town employee if his family has been here a long time but it's almost an impossibility." (Note, he was speaking of 1950 when the Yankees had moved out; many of the old Yankees whose families had been there eight, nine, or ten generations would not necessarily have had relatives who worked for the town. But among the Irish in Watertown—they being the particular upper blue collar, etcetera, types they were—the statement was entirely correct.) The Citizens' leader then went ahead to argue that if the Homeowners insistence won out and town employees and their relatives were forbidden to take part in the representative town meeting, that "would end up by disenfranchising nearly all the people. I'd like to know if that is constitutional." Nevertheless, during the early and mid 50s, in both Arlington and Brookline, (near-by towns governed by representative town meetings)—fearing the kind of sentiment which developed in Watertown, town employees deliberately moved to reduce the representation of themselves and their families from town meeting. This was certainly easier in Brookline, probably easier in Arlington, because they do not have quite the same ethnic-class-status mix as Watertown. Had it been done in Watertown, it might very likely, although of course this is impossible to prove, have materially reduced quality and competence in town meeting committees and debates. Perhaps, the move actually did reduce the competence of the Arlington representative town meeting?

3

Meaningful History — History as Experienced by The Participants In the Conflict

The history of Watertown in the formal sense is of course a history which traces back to the Englishmen who settled and incorporated the town in the 1630s. Their descendants or descendants of men like them became the old Yankees who were frequently referred to in discussion of town matters. Although this early history was more likely to be mentioned on formal occasions, it is unlikely—except for the institution of the town meeting and related institutional patterns—that it had much effect on those who had been active in town affairs. Probably, no one active in the conflict knew or remembered that John Oldham, one of the founders of Watertown in the 1630s, in setting up the town tried to arrange matters so that it would not be aristocratic, hierarchically run, as in his view, Plymouth was (sic!). Although Watertown genealogists in the nineteenth century had boasted about Watertown being the mother town of the West—so many people moved through Watertown or left it to settle the Northwest Territories, they said—matters of this sort, if referred to at all, were more apt to be mentioned in the schools than in discussions about town affairs or local history.

The generalized conception of the town meeting as a democracy and the general notion of the right of the citizen to pass upon his tax rate—the history of the 1760s and 1770s—had, unquestionably, a considerable effect upon the new migrants into town, (that is, the migrants of the late 40s and early 50s). But they lacked, naturally enough, any specific sense of the immediately preceding history of Watertown. No Homeowner leader, to my recollection, ever referred to the happenings in Watertown of the preceding half century.

On the other hand, the town meeting members and the town employees and their supporters constantly, in my interviews with them at least, referred to the preceding twenty-five or fifty years of town political conflict. The bulk of town meeting members and employees were Irish-American in the fourth generation, for the most part, from workers who had come to the Hood Rubber Company or to factories in Waltham or Cambridge. They looked back to a series of conflicts which were remembered in almost epic terms, between themselves as young men or their fathers on the one hand, and some leading old Yankees on the other. For the most part, in a manner entirely consonant with the stereotype of the Irish-American political battler, these earlier political battles were reported as a joy to experience and to behold. Prior to 1933, some of the issues involved welfare expenditures, issues that must have been at the time vital for some people. However, no one I interviewed in Watertown itself ever referred to the substance of these battles, there was never any mention of the issues at stake.

Said one who had been an active participant in the battles between the old Yankee leaders and their opponents: "It was all in the spirit of good, clean fun. . ." Remembered another: "Of course, people slanged each other. I can remember Wilfred Pacquet (who later served for many years as a judge) who was then Democratic leader, and some of the Republicans, calling each other everything under the sun . . . but it was like lawyers in a courtroom, either they lost or they won, and then they'd joke with each other. But it's quite different now. . ."

It is irrelevant for understanding the situation in the 50s whether the "good, clean fun" of earlier years was accurately remembered. The most prominent of the old Yankee leaders, according to a story several times told, some twenty-five or thirty years back, found an outhouse placed in his yard—as a response to some town meeting stratagems. He may not have thought this good, clean fun. It may have been that there never was such an insult by outhouse. The point is that these later leaders in town politics—the people who for reasons to be described had taken over the town—had a notion and a conception, based upon such recollections, as to how town fights would be carried on. Anthropologists have distinguished between history-as-it-actually-happened and history-as-it-gets-meaning-in-the-lives-of-those-who-believe-or – assert-something-happened.[19] It does not matter for purposes of understanding these events whether the latter was also the former.

But it is important to recognize that the new migrants into town, the people who moved in in the 40s and 50s, lacked this background of experienced recollection. When, as reported below, nine inspectors from town departments—none of them requested or expected—came in just one day to the home of one of the Homeowner leaders, they did not regard this as good, clean fun in the traditional sense, but as harassment. When a policemen ticketed Homeowner cars, and explained that he was doing a police duty—protecting himself and his fellow-policemen from being robbed of their wage rises by the Homeowners—it was exactly in the spirit of the old town political battles, as remembered. But since these particular cars had never been ticketed before, although formally they should have been (there was a general understanding in town that people could park cars near their own houses, even though this was a technical violation of ordinances), the Homeowners regarded it not as a joke, but as iniquitous.

Town meeting members, for the most part, and town employees played out political battles, constantly remembering a presence that was no longer there. Many people referred to the old Yankees—but nearly all the old Yankee families had, in fact, moved out of town. Actually, the old Yankees seem to have consisted of two different categories, sometimes overlapping, to be sure. One consisted of families which had lived in Watertown for generations. Several members of such families, during the early part of the twentieth century, were, clearly, town leaders—figures to be remembered. But they left few heirs in Watertown. What happened was that their children and grandchildren became part of a regional and national professional and business group (the phenomenon has been described accurately enough by John P. Marquand in his mythical but very realistic Clyde). Watertown, although attractive enough, does not have any of the special aura which occasionally has kept a few members of old families in Marblehead or Salem or on Beacon Hill. Although some members of such families simply moved over the line to new developments in adjoining Weston, they were lost to Watertown. But the majority, as is true of every old New England town with competent, bright, Yankee families, scattered over the country.[20] And the few descendants of such families who stayed in Watertown were generally regarded as weak twigs off strong trees, perhaps correctly, perhaps because their own self-definition (as people who had not made it on a larger cosmopolitan or national scale) would basically tend to lead to their being demeaned.

The other sort of "old Yankee" in the latter part of the 19th and the early part of the 20th century was the Yankee who worked in a management position at the Hood Rubber Company, or a few other manufacturing plants in and around Watertown, *or* who owned or managed retail business in Watertown Square. But, as has been true all over the country, these industries, both manufacturing and retail, by 1950 had come under the control of national organisations;[21] the Hood, for instance, was simply a subsidiary of a midWestern manufacturer. As local businessmen, living in Watertown, managers and owners apparently played a prominent part in town affairs; certainly, as men remembered, they took stands and gave advice. But as the firms for which they worked became parts of larger national entities, several things coincided to decrease their participation in Watertown affairs. First, the national owners would be, in the nature of the case, more likely to criticize them for getting into local "squabbles" and making (possibly) enemies, than reward them for being good citizens of the community. (It should be remembered that all this took place before the business in government emphasis of 1960, which, however, probably would not have made much difference.[22]) Second, if these new managers lived in Watertown, they had much less personal incentive to concern themselves with it: a future promotion or a lateral movement or a demotion would be likely to see them moving somewhere else, hundreds of miles away. And, third, the automobile, the new developments west of Watertown, and the fact that Watertown increasingly had become a town in which high-status people did not live, meant that few of these managers in fact lived in Watertown.

It should be pointed out, in view of the emphasis upon history-as-experienced-above, that the distinction between the two types of old Yankees was not made by anybody with whom I talked. It is purely an analytic product of reflection.

However, in many ways the memory of the old Yankees dominated the scene. A prominent, as it happened, Armenian spoke of them as "a governor like on an automobile", something now lacking in the town which "the newer generations" (ethnic stocks) have not yet produced. "They (the newer ethnic stocks) don't seem to have the pride in their town and their state that the old Yankees had." Among the Irish-Americans, active in town affairs, there was a distinct note of admiration for these old Yankees, sometimes combined with a feeling of contempt for their few remaining descendants in town. There was, in fact, an ambivalance towards the memory of the old Yankees: on the one hand this sense of strength, leadership, and because the Irish had now taken their place in town, identification. So, the Irish-Americans cherished the idea of a well-run, businesslike town. On the other hand, there was a recollection of the old Yankees as scrooges, totally lacking in charity, who would take the bread out of the mouths of starving children. This was most eloquently stated by a man active in advising and helping the various associations concerned with town affairs at the state level, who lived and had lived most of his long life a few blocks outside Watertown. "New England town government" he said, "was said forty or fifty years ago to be the purest form of democracy, but it was. . . as I can tell you from my own observation very impure. . .It did, of course, provide a place where every character could shoot his mouth off." (So much for democratic participation!) "Conservative government, typical of such towns as Watertown (then) above everything else consisted of low expenditures. . . the suburban towns sponging off Boston and Cambridge. . .The (local) Welfare Department would despise all the laws. . .The town Welfare agent would pull every trick in the book not to give people what the state law said they should have." He then went ahead and described how two of the (in men's recollections in the 50s) more than life-size figures in Watertown in the

20s and 30s were "money-hungry, miserly. . ." One of them "in 1931 wanted to cut down town employees some ridiculous figure (in wages). . .I think it was 50 percent and that was typical of all of them."

It seemed in the 50s to depend which button one pressed, which stimulus one set in motion, whether the old Yankees were remembered as misers in this sense or as powerful people—whether the similarity in being powerful or the dissimilarity in being generous came to attention—among town officials. The Homeowners by their insistence on cutting down town employee salaries of course reminded the Irish-Americans, who now ran the town and were also to a considerable degree town employees, of the miserliness of the old Yankees. I surmise that a good deal of the bitterness which the new people, the Homeowners, evoked was in reality because they reactivated the hostility which had been felt and passed on towards the more "miserly" of the old Yankees. But, of course, the Homeowners had none of the impression of leadership nor the skill at playing political games which had made the old Yankees also admirable to the Irish-Americans.

One phrase was constantly used by the long-time town residents—mostly, of course, supporters of town employees. They spoke of people who "know" or "knew" Watertown. Unfortunately, at the time I did not appreciate its full significance, but it evidently was a code word; a similar one, I found in the U. S. House of Representatives in the early 50s, was to say of some member "he loves the House." Included in this "knowing" were a whole complex of meanings: awareness of the recent history of the town, knowledge of what the town employees did for the town, appreciation of the kinds of political battles the town was accustomed to fighting. But in a broader sense, perhaps "knowing Watertown" meant that one was a member of the Watertown community—and much of Watertown was a community. In this, again, it differed from adjoining Belmont; in the forty-two years during which I lived in Belmont, off and on, I never heard any similar phrase; for even in 1931, Belmont had stopped being a community but was rather simply a set of houses. "Knowing Watertown" has in a way the significance which alumni songs, cheers, and self congratulations had in some American colleges before the war at least, and it did serve to differentiate Watertown from many other suburban towns. In the nature of the case, the Homeowners could not "know" Watertown–not at least unless they were unusually sympathetic or anthropologically oriented. However, it should be pointed out that a couple of old-timers did draw a contrast between the Homeowners who violated the rules of the game and "the ADA faction" which did not, which was perfectly acceptable in old Watertown terms. The "ADA faction" (Americans for Democratic Action) consisted, I take it, of a few liberal people of the sort who more characteristically would have lived in Newton, across the river, professionals, who by some accident, or because housing was cheaper in Watertown, had ended up there. (Any one knowing Watertown more recently in the 70s will realize that more liberal professionals, not necessarily ADA members, have moved into Watertown since 1960).

4

Further Setting of the Stage

It would be misleading to suppose that Watertown was all Irish-American. A number of Italians had moved in around the turn of the century; on the whole, fewer of them than Irish were active in town politics. Following the great Armenian migration to the United States as a result of the massacres during World War I, Armenians came to Watertown in sufficient quantity so that Watertown was in the 50s widely said to be the largest Armenian town in the United States, east of Fresno, California. On the whole, the Italians supported the Irish and the Democrats, while the Armenians leaned towards the Yankees and the Republicans, or so people thought. Subsequently, in the 70s, the development of emphasis upon Armenian records of the massacres, similar to the Jewish concern for the Holocaust, originated from Watertown.

In the period following World War II, at the same time as those who became Homeowners moved in, a substantial number of Protestant Canadians came into town, probably for the same reasons. But at no time, during my interviewing, did I ever encounter anybody from Canada or of Canadian origin.

Altogether, by the midfifties, Watertown had a population of about 40,000 persons. Unlike many other Massachusetts towns, elections to local office were often bitterly contested. Much excitement sometimes revolved around contests for such obscure posts as Tree Warden. And, unlike the great majority of Massachusetts towns, contests for town office were, often actually, usually by reputation, on a party basis; in most Massachusetts towns elections for local office were and are genuinely nonpartisan. It is worth noting that for this reason some people interpreted the whole Homeowners controversy as part of a Republican plot against the Democrats. This seems to me extremely inaccurate (with the one brief and tenuous exception noted at the appropriate part of the chronological account). In the event nearly all the prominent Republicans in town lined up with the Democrats against the Homeowners.

An interesting, and misleading, description of Watertown was given to me by several people in Cambridge who had been engaged in studying parts of Greater Boston. They said "Watertown is particularly homogenous (as compared with other Boston suburbs)." Formally this was true; but psychologically, and for the political purposes at hand, it was false. It was formally true if one looked at categories like income, educatinal attainment, and employment of Watertowners in the 1950s. Belmont, Boston, Cambridge, Newton, and Waltham, the five immediately adjoining communities, certainly showed a much larger variation in such categories; so did places like Burlington and Wakefield. Going through Watertown, one would find none of the wealthy houses and few of the rather run-down three-deckers characteristic of different sections of Belmont. Newton probably had a higher proportion of juveniles apt to make trouble just as it had a far higher proportion of wealthy persons. Watertown had (so far as anybody knew or commented) no blacks and few Jews; other towns of course had blacks and Jews.

All this was true; but to say that this betokens homogeneity is to say that the artifacts or categories which scholars typically use for their analyses are indices of the psychopolitical variations and controversies within a community. If one used controversis about which people felt strongly on issues of local politics, Watertown would have far less homogeity, conformity, whatever one wants to call it than Belmont or Winchester or numerous other towns in Massachusetts. It may be that "basically" values were far more heterogenous in Belmont or Waltham than in Watertown; but at the manifest level, differences in valuation as experienced by the participants were probably, historically and currently (in 1953), greater in Watertown than in many other towns. Granted that of the twenty-three suburbs north and west of Boston, Watertown in the 50s was most nearly confined to craftsmen, senior clerks, moderate level salesmen, skilled blue collar workers. The academic persons with whom Watertown was discussed drew the inference in a neat phrasing that Watertown therefore had "a rhythm of continuity and community of occupation which might well promote a consensus in outlook and make town meeting government workable . . ." There are two difficulties with this assumption. One is the theme of F.G. Bailey's *Gifts and Poison: The Politics of Reputation.*[23] "This is about people competing to remain equal . . . Sometimes, the threat (to equality) is imagined and, like an armaments race, the whole affair seems wasteful, and therefore tragic . . . The fight between equals tells only of frustration and the waste of human endeavor." The threat to equality in Watertown might be regarded as, on the one hand, from the town to the Homeowners; the rising tax rate threatened the hardwon equality in housing between old Watertowners and new. And once awareness of this threat took place, it called attention to another threat: the old Watertowners who ran the town had more influence and power than the new incomers, even though they were approximately each other's equal in social status. But, on the other hand, the town employees did regard themselves as threatened, both socially and economically, by the Homeowners. The Homeowners threatened their economic status by trying to deny them and their kinfolk and colleagues raises designed to compensate for the increased cost of living, due to inflation. And when the Homeowners broadened the issue to an attack on the participation of town employees and their relatives in town meeting they threatened the claims to status and worth of the latter; for the latter very honestly felt that they had an earned right to run things, because they had developed skills which enabled them to do so. And the Homeowners, from their standpoint, who did not "know Watertown" could not legitimately take over from them. It goes beyond the realm of the provable but perhaps the frequent citation by the town employees of the Old Yankees was self-reassuring, saying in effect "We are not saying that everybody who disagrees with us can not run things. But they have to have the skills and know-how which we have. These Old Yankees had it; the Homeowners have not." And, it is likely that Bailey's approach is correct; the very slight differences in status between the old Watertowners and the Homeowners probably added bitterness to the fight.

But there is a second way of looking at the situation: there were real differences between the insiders and the newcomer Homeowners. The insiders had a genuine sentiment about Watertown as a community; to the newcomers, Watertown was largely a happenstance. The insiders treasured their town know-how and related political skills; to the newcomers, insofar as they recognized these skills, they were devices for "screwing" people. And, perhaps equally important, is a third point which has not been mentioned yet: observers of Massachusetts local government during the thirties and forties report that one of the big changes in attitude was the shift from local government *jobs* to local government *careers.* That is, policemen, firemen, public health workers, librarians, would in 1925 have regarded themselves as having a job; by 1955, they felt themselves engaged in a career. There were abilities and competences which they had acquired; there was equipment which they knew how to manage. If not strictly professional, they were feeling their way towards professionalism. There was a good deal of shared recognition and discovery here; many people not on the Fire Department boasted to me of the advanced methods of resuscitation (for heart attacks and the like) which the Watertown Fire Department employed. But, on the whole, this career service orientation was much more important to the town employees than to the newcomers, although the difference between the two groups was not as great here as in regard to community sentiment and political skills.

Moving Into Watertown: the Newcomers From Whom Came the Homeowners

In large measure, no doubt because the old Yankees left, during the period from 1946 to 1955, there was a real change in Watertown's population. They were replaced, so to speak, by clerks, skilled craftsmen, and others living on moderate incomes, from Boston, or Cambridge, or often having recently come into metropolitan Boston. It is important to point out, also, that there was some new housing in Watertown (though not developments of the sort found in Weston), and that many Irish also moved out. Also, some older, poorer Watertowners moved into housing projects, leaving houses available for incomers.

It was a definite step into amenity to leave Boston or Cambridge for Watertown. Watertown was a definitely better choice for people moving into the metropolis than these cities. Property cost substantially less than in atttactive areas of Cambridge or Boston or Newton or Belmont. In general, of the near-in suburbs, Watertown had attractions for lower middle income people, which could only be matched by Arlington, and public transportation to much of Watertown was rather better than to much of Arlington. It was cheap because it lacked eclat and had lost its rural charm. A vastly oversimplified pair of terms seems to be applicable to most of those who moved in during this period: "worthy, politically naive." But they had, many of them, expectations about what a town would be like as contrasted with the "corrupt" cities (Boston and Cambridge) from which many of them came. They were also people with some energy, willing to go to considerable effort if challenged. Many, probably most, of them did not have many associational or kinfolk ties in Watertown itself, so that they could more readily spend a fair amount of energy on a new organization if it appealed to them.

The most important characteristic of these new Watertowners was, however, financial. Most of them had committed as much as they had in the way of resources in order to get a house for themselves, a better neighborhood for their children. Through the Korean War, at least, and perhaps a bit longer, they were able to meet the payments and demands of the new residence; some of them could count on overtime, others were making pretty good commissions and so on. But, after the Korean War was over, things changed for them—and for the town.

5

Why Was Watertown the Scene of Bitter Conflict

So, finally, we begin to get to the story. During the 1946–53 period, town employees came to face a major problem. The purchasing power of wages shrank, because of the first inflation in 1946 to 1947, and then because of the Korean War. Few readers of these pages will remember clearly that in the 30s and even during the War, being a fireman or a cop was a "good job." The pay was steady and secure; one could look forward where civil service or equivalent prevailed, as in Watertown, to a decent pension; and the work and service performed were respectable—becoming as pointed out above, more and more of a career. Among members of the social classes from which policemen, firemen, and the like were recruited it was indeed an extremely good job.

The inflation changed the economic aspects of this. Towns and cities were slow to raise wages to match it. Watertown was not by any means the most generous of Massachusetts communities and as pointed out below may have been the last one to incorporate the inflation adjustments of the Korean War into its base wages. In practical terms, for older men and women, this was important; because the pension was calculated in Massachusetts on the wage base, and no credit was given for inflation adjustments (cops and firemen of course could retire at fifty).

During World War II, of course, town and city employees saw industrial workers race ahead of them in wages. But there was a universally admitted national emergency, and almost everybody expected a post war depression like that of 1921. This depression did not develop; and the strength which industrial unions had acquired in 1933 to 1945 meant that many industrial workers kept or even raised their wartime wage levels. This could have been tolerated, perhaps, except for two additional factors:

> (1) The Korean War repeated the experience of inflation, and in one way created more difficulty, psychologically, for town employees. During the War itself, those particularly handicapped by or resentful of industrial wage boosts knew they could get better paying jobs in the war emergency or private sector, if they wished. This was not necessarily the case in 1951 to 1953, because the Korean War did not result in full mobilization, and
>
> (2) during the post-war period, there was, due to GI Bill and other such factors, some reversal of the career value attached to town employment. When younger brothers, cousins, or sons went to college and got professional jobs, the status of police and fire and so on became less. It seems highly probable that some of the irritability of the uniformed branches during the 50s may have represented or been influenced by this relative deprivation.

These factors were, to some degree, present in most greater Boston suburbs. But they did not lead in any of them to a serious and bitter conflict. Why did Watertown differ? First, there was no one in Watertown who was above the battle and could advise that wages be jacked up or held down and be listened to, as there was in Belmont, for example, Second, the particular people, the newcomers who moved into Watertown, were more adversely affected by the rising tax rate (which they attributed to the wage raises)—it represented a bigger bite—than in the case of people who moved into the more affluent suburbs. In the third place, there were accidents of personality, among the police leaders in the episode which launched the battle, and in the cases of Miles Robinson and Treasurer Robert Hagopian mentioned below. More important than any of these, the underlying statute was fuzzy and ambiguous (although there were other underlying statutes which were fuzzy and ambiguous, too). But I suspect that the most important thing may have been that in Watertown, unlike most other suburbs, town meeting members and town employees had for several years been able to regard themselves as "the town." They themselves were the people they saw who both worked and lived in Watertown. The newcomers largely worked elsewhere, were not there during the day, were not active in, for example, recreational affairs and the like, and until the episodes about to be described, were not conspicuous. In Belmont, the town employees did not live in town; in Brookline, the much greater concern of the Jewish professionals for decent local government meant they at least were seen and heard at town hall; in Winchester there appeared to be a much greater participation in recreational and other affairs of people not politically active in town, and far more of the new immigrants carried ties with other immigrants and with Winchesterites than was the case in Watertown. And so on. So, Watertown town employees had come, apparently, to regard themselves as the effective community, in a way which was less likely elsewhere. People in such a position are more apt to resent challenge and criticism than those less convinced of their own place at the center.[24]

6

Employee Pay Raises and Resistance Thereto

In the spring of 1953, the regular annual meeting of the limited town meeting raised all employee salaries $100 per annum, but it refused to approve an additional raise of $210 for policemen and firemen. The request for a special raise for police and fire had been referred, according to correct procedure, to the standing committee on personnel matters, called the Advisory Board of Review, which had disapproved that request 8 to 1. The policemen and firemen argued for special treatment by saying (a) their jobs were particularly dangerous (b) they were mostly (unlike some other town employees who were women) married men.[25]

However, the following July, four months later, the policemen and firemen saw another opportunity to get consideration of the special raise for them. Because the federal and state governments had arranged to eliminate areawide rent control, under the provisions of the Massachusetts statute, then in effect, on rent control, a *special* town meeting was called to decide whether the town itself wished to have its own rent control agency. The town officials, following the normal practice of executives, faced with a special legislative meeting, tried to keep off of the warrant (in essence the agenda document) all items which had been acted on at the regular meeting four months before. After all, a special meeting in July would necessarily find a good many town meeting members away on vacation and unable to attend. But a procedure existed by which a given number of petitioners can request that an item be added to the warrant, even if not put there by town officials. The police and fire were easily able to get the requisite number of petitioners—the item was added—and at the special town meeting at which two-fifths of the members were absent (only 185 attending), the additional $210 raise for police and fire was approved.[26]

Since both the Advisory Board of Review and the Town Finance Committee had disapproved the raise, their members, and others in town, immediately argued that letting town employees use the town meeting to overrule the standing committees was totally wrong. Of course, there is no more a legal requirement that the town meeting follow standing committees than there is that the Federal or State House of Representatives follow their standing committees; but traditional practice in many Massachusetts towns, and in Watertown was (or was believed to have been) to follow the decisions of standing committees.

A prominent old Yankee, Miles Robinson, was at that time a member of the Finance Committee. In some ways, he was regarded as almost unique, a survivor of the vanished area which many looked back to with mixed feelings, as described above. His father and his grandfather were remembered as Titans of town government, tough men who had led the fight for, as you chose to see it, economy or parsimony or downright miserliness. Whether this recollection was correct, it determined the way many people looked at Robinson, and it may well have determined the corresponding picture of Robinson himself as a weak and ineffective twig off a strong tree.

In any case, Robinson was prominent among those who resorted to a provision of the statute of 1919 under which the Watertown town meeting operated. This provision specified, partly because the whole idea of a *limited* town meeting in 1919 seemed a kind of contradiction in terms, that a referendum could be held on the actions of the limited town meeting. In fact, for understandable philosophical or tactical[27] reasons, the basic statute is confusingly drafted; it refers at points to "the town meeting," meaning the results of the referendum, and at other points to the representative town meeting as the town meeting. This is much as though, in some state, the referendum or the initiative should be called the legislature, while referring to the legislature by that same word!

The referendum had only twice before in recollection been used, once on a matter of interest to only a small section of the town. But, now after thirty-four years of practical disuse, those town influentials on the Advisory Board of Review and the Finance Committee, decided to use it to demonstrate that the *consensus* of the town was against the rump special town meeting of July, 1953. In essence, the police and fire had pulled a fast one, employing the always risky procedure of getting a decision approved by a sparse meeting which might not be approved by a full one. So, the senior town influentials on Finance and the Advisory Board reached into the closet to, as you chose to see it, pull a dirty trick in return, or in Schattschneider's terms[28] to enlarge the arena of conflict, or in their own terms, to reintroduce the original conception of town meeting. But, of course, it was an old conception with a big difference—conducted as a political campaign rather than with the discussion, which, at its best, accompanies a genuine town meeting.[29]

The leaders of the policemen and firemen were quoted, quite freely, by the local newspapers to the effect that they were sure of winning if there was a small vote—meaning that town employees, postmen, and other people familiar with politics and town affairs always vote and would support the raise. The wisdom of publicizing such an analysis may be questioned within a society which makes a good deal of democratic participation. The vote was, however, not extremely small—considerably larger than predicted by either side—although by standards of absolute participation it was low. One-third of the electorate (33 percent) voted; and the raise for police and fire was ratified 3664 to 2849. The effect on the tax rate was slight—forty cents per thousand assessed valuation; the maximum salaries of the lowest paid grades of patrolmen and fire privates were raised to $3,660 a year, plus a cost-of-living allowance based on official (Federal) cost-of-living figures. So far as one can see, for the time and place, these figures were neither terribly mean nor at all generous—comparatively speaking. Secretaries with some experience and fair skill but no college training in adjoining cities made higher wages; taking into account the cost-of-living bonus, a good many college instructors then made less (to be sure, only for nine months work, but they had some years of training, if that be relevant). In 1954, at the regular town meeting, the police and fire got further fringe benefits, now generally regarded as decent, then reasonably common but not at all standard: a five day (instead of a five and a half day) week, group life insurance, and additional, compensatory, time off, if their duty fell on certain specified holidays.

In 1955, the partisan factor in town politics became more important for this reason; all the town offices up for election were carried by the Democrats, the first time in many years that one party had won such a clear-cut victory. However, since members of the Finance Committee and the Advisory Board of Review serve three-year overlapping terms, they did not fully reflect the shift.

In the Finance Committee report for 1955, Miles Robinson, serving that year as Chairman, argued that town expenditures had increased from 1950 to 1955 substantially more than the increase in valuation of property. I say "argued" because the statement, though literally true, was not particularly illuminating: for one thing, the town assessments depended upon a number of fortuitous factors (for instance, a man like Robinson himself, unless on incredibly bad terms with the assessors, was in current Watertown practice less likely to have his house assessed at full value, in those days, than would have been the case had some stranger bought it; in other words, assessment was an artifact of other factors). Also, one might well argue that the choice of the year 1950 was unreasonable because services had gone up from 1935 to 1955 and that twenty years span might be more relevant, and so on, and so on. In any case, Robinson's point was that in fiscal year 1955, the town spent one and two-tenths million dollars more than in 1950. However, nearly half of this[30] (his figures did not make the exact proportion clear) was due to an increase in the budget for school purposes; the town meeting, under Massachusetts law and practice, has no control over (most) school costs—the School Committee can and does appeal directly to the State, if its demands are not met.[31] (And the School Committee, in many towns, including Watertown, has a different effective constituency than the town meeting, within the town). Almost one-twelfth of the total increase was due to debt service on capital construction, already committed. But about $275,000 per year *of the increase was* attributable to the item classified as "protection of persons and property," that is, police and fire. Robinson further complained that although there had been no increase in fire hazards and no significant increase in population, the police department was nine men larger, the fire department twenty-two men larger than in 1950 (there was no serious effort to compare Watertown with any national standards or other communities). The implication was that this item had grown so much because of a "swollen" work force and unduly expensive rates of pay and fringe benefits.

Nevertheless, on the warrant, there appeared a series of requests for employee pay raises. Almost every one of them was in fact passed at the regular spring town meeting in 1955, "over the objection" as was recorded "of the Finance Committee and the Advisory Board of Review." It was a remarkable occasion: the legislative body took the bit in its hands, bucked the standing committees, and ultimately was swept away by its exhilaration at finding out how easy it was. One after another employee groups were voted pay raises. Late in the meeting the Town's Tree Warden, Thomas Morley, got up and said that, although he had not come to the meeting with any intention of asking for anything, this year, "but since you were so kind as to give others a raise, I am asking a slight increase," of $400. Amidst laughter and protests, this sum was voted to the Tree Warden; the next week, the Town meeting gave him, more substantially, two additional employees for his department.

The *Watertown Sun* and *Press* reported these events as showing fiscal irresponsibility and grabbiness; I believe (though nobody remembered clearly by 1958) that the radio similarly reported what happened; and the whole way it was handled, by such people as Morley, was not, to put it mildly, good public relations. Yet, in fact, town services had increased, the town was only for the most part providing the same kind of fringe benefits which the State and the Federal government and many towns and cities already took pretty much for granted, and the pay scale had certainly not kept up with the increased cost of living.

One of the difficulties was the (unfounded) feeling that sooner or later inflation would reverse itself. The town employees had a cost-of-living figure written into their wages; but they were worried about it because it did not count towards pension and retirement. Economizers, actuaries, accountants, Finance Committee members felt that to write the cost-of-living bonus into the permanent pay scale would make wages more controllable and predictable. So, it was agreed in 1955 that a committee to study the cost of living increment wage problem should be set up.

This special committee reported to the Finance Committee and the Advisory Board of Review. These two committees then recommended in 1956 a new salary plan to the regular town meeting. There were two major provisions in this new plan:

(1) The *base* salary figure would in the first place be changed to include the 12 percent cost-of-living allowance, generally received by town employees already, to allow for inflation. This did not as such actually increase anybody's take-home pay; but it did (a) provide employees with a higher wage base on which to provide for their retirement pensions[32] and (b) give a greater feeling of fixity to the cost-of-living allowances.

(2) Second, an *additional* 6 percent or $250, whichever was larger, would be incorporated into the base figure; for most employees this was an actual increase, as well as of course increasing the retirement base still further.

This development and subsequent developments through December, 1957, involved a good many complexities, not all necessary for our main themes, and difficult to follow chronologically. Some readers will probably find the table below helpful in checking the story.[33]

CHRONOLOGICAL CHART–PAGE I

(based on stories in Watertown newspapers)[34]

PAGE I December 13, 1955: School Committee accepts plan of Advisory Board of Review, making permanent the cost-of-living allowance of 12 percent plus additional 6 percent or $250, whichever was higher, for School employees. (The previous week the School Committee had favored simply giving $400 increase in teacher maxima). This was very important because the School Committee is the largest employer of personnel in town, and perhaps $4 of the $10 increase was due to this decision of the Committee's, AND the town meeting has no authority over (most) school salaries.

PAGE 6 Jan. 10, 1956: Advisory Board plan as described in text made public; it also included a provision for hourly paid workers, and specific raises for various classes of employees, such as senior clerk-typist, billing machine operator, purchasing agent, building custodians, fire lieutenants and captains, and the creation of two types of new positions.

PAGE 1 March 1: Finance Committee indicated tax rate will rise $5 to $8 per thousand assessed valuation.

PAGE 1 March 5: Majority of Finance Committee votes for Advisory Board of Review Plan. Chairman of Finance Committee estimates tax rate will go up $8.60 per thousand.

PAGE 1 March 26: Preliminary grade changes (up) voted by limited town meeting.

PAGE 1 April 2: Salary plan as above approved, 147–92.

PAGE 1 April 16: At end of town meeting, raise of $8.60 to $9.60 per thousand seen.

PAGE 1 April 20: Petition is filed for referendum on salary plan, on adjustments, on elected officials salaries, for indefinite postponement of cost-of-living appropriation.

PAGE 1 May 3: Selectmen declare petition in legal form, set date of referendum election, but declare they believe referendum will not be valid authority for them to supercede decision of town meeting. Petitioners form Homeowners and Tenants Protective Association.

PAGE 1 May 5: Citizens Committee for the Preservation of the Town Meeting Form of Government (town employees and their supporters) formed.

PAGE 1 May 31: Homeowners Organization reports filing of suit in equity asking injunction against the settling of tax rate; Town Counsel's immediate reaction is that since the referendum applies only to Article 29 (cost-of-living-raises) and not to Article 3 (appropriations) of the warrant for the limited town meeting of the spring, the tax rate will be unaffected.

PAGE 1 June 7: But, on subsequent reflection, Town Counsel notes that another aspect of the referendum might affect the tax rate and recommends delay in setting it.

PAGE 1 June 13, 1956: Referendum in which 54 percent of the electorate vote; salary hikes rejected by 2-to-1 margin.

PAGE 1 June 14: Selectmen announce that nevertheless on advice of town counsel they will continue the higher rate of pay.

and June 14: Tax rate of $61.80 is set by officials, based on limited town meeting vote (regardless of referendum), a hike of $10.40 over previous year.

PAGE 1 June 15: Town employees in fact are paid base pay only (minus accustomed cost of living) by disbursing officer.

PAGE 1 June 25: Town Treasurer confirms his refusal to pay higher rates or cost of living; will pay base only. Selectmen set August 6 as date for special town meeting.

PAGE 1 July 2: Police retain attorney in dispute, employees continue to receive only base pay (in fact that is the referendum cut their pay 12 percent for the time being).

PAGE 1 July 12: Attorney for employees will file suit in equity; Homeowners leaders file four articles for special town meeting including restoration of cost-of-living allowance (effort at compromise).

PAGE 1 July 17: Employees' attorney files suit in equity in Superior Court, petition for declaratory judgment. Selectment reinsert all salary articles voted on at annual meeting on request of town employees in warrant for special meeting.

PAGE 1 July 26: Advisory Board votes in favor of salary articles rejected by voters in referendum.

PAGE 1 August 2: Finance Committee concurs with Advisory Board.

PAGE 1 August 9: Town meeting of August 6 restores disputed salary plan of spring by vote of 179–63 (e.g. nullifies the referendum). Treasurer announces he will pay the higher salaries unless a new referendum petition is filed.

PAGE 1 August 16: Second referendum petition reported as filed August 10. Selectmen on August 13 reported as requesting withdrawal of this referendum petition saying the only legitimate subject included therein is salaries for elected officials.

PAGE 1 August 23: Homeowners seek writ of mandamus to compel referendum election. On advice of State officials, Treasurer states he will pay base pay only.

PAGE 1 September 6: In order to avoid confusion, Homeowners agree to withdraw item on salaries of elected officials.

PAGE 1 September 13: Meeting of September 11 in effort to work out compromise reported unsuccessful.

PAGE 1 September 20: Employees vote of September 14 rejecting strike reported.

PAGE 1 September 27: Pay cases argued September 25 in Superior Court.

PAGE 1 October 18: Superior Court finds for petitioners (town employees) and orders they be paid full amount voted in spring; dismisses Homeowners petition for a referendum.

PAGE 1 October 25: Pay raises held up during pendency of appeal period.

PAGE 1 November 1: Homeowners announce intention to appeal; Treasurer to pay raises unless stopped by courts.

PAGE 1 November 22: $200,000 in pay raises (largely back pay) paid to employees. Temporary injunction to halt this payment was denied by the courts on November 15.

PAGE 1 January 17, 1957: Homeowners leadership sends protest to "schools" on teachers having influenced the situation adversely to Homeowners during referendum contest.

PAGE 1 January 24: Teachers ask retraction from Homeowners.

PAGE 1 January 31: School Board holds extraordinary Saturday meeting and asks apology from Homeowners.

PAGE 1 February 7: Parent-Teacher-Association Council supports teachers by *one-vote margin* against Homeowners.

PAGE 1 February 28: Homeowners announce slate of town meeting candidates.

PAGE 1 March 7: Homeowners "win" 77 out of 106 town meeting vacancies in March 4 election.

PAGE 8 March 14: Homeowners urge support of Finance Committee Recommendations.

PAGE 1 March 27: Homeowners favor incinerator proposal of Department of Public Works, etc. (costing money).

PAGE 1 December 18: Supreme Court reverses Superior Court.

7

What Was the Tax Raise Really Due To?

The Advisory Board of Review and the Finance Committee had, of course, changed somewhat in composition between 1955 and 1956: the new members were more sympathetic to the town employees. And even those members who wanted to favor more economy had come away from the 1955 meeting so thoroughly beaten, they did not want a recap of the same battle. And third, some of the long-time economizers felt that in fact they were putting something over on the town employees by writing in the 6 percent figure, as they felt convinced that the cost of living would shortly go up more than 6 percent, but that the town employees could not then reopen the issue. (They were, see below, quite right; everybody else was wrong!)

The 12 percent incorporation was approved without argument; it is worth noting as showing Watertown's relative lack of generosity to town employees that, according to the uncontested statement of the Chairman of the Advisory Board of Review, every other town in the state had previously incorporated the war—Korean War—cost-of-living allowances into the retirement base. There was considerable argument on the 6 percent figure, but it was finally approved by a vote of 147 to 92.[35]

The assessors had, shortly prior to this vote, but partly in expectation of it, indicated, in conjunction with the Selectmen, that the tax rate would jump about $10 per $1,000 of assessed valuation. The chronological listing of stories in the press and the whole climate of argument almost certainly suggested that this entire tax hike was due to the reclassification of town employees under the plan just described. It was fairly obvious that many of the Homeowners leaders whom I interviewed started out by believing this, and, by the time they found they were in error, already had a movement and a following. "We definitely did explain to people" said several of them to me, more or less jointly, "that if these raises went through there would be a $10 raise in the tax rate. Later we began to realize that it was nearer $5, because the school teachers (actually most school employees) whom we could not touch took $5. But within no time the $10 figure was all over town." Still later, these leaders came to realize that in fact the salary raises probably did not explain more than $2 of the tax increase.

What else was the hike due to? First, the School Committee had adopted for its employees the plan of 12 percent and 6 percent above described; but, under Massachusetts law and practice, the town meeting had no authority over the salaries of school employees, engaged bona fide in the educational process.[36] The School Committee sets its own budget, and, accordingly, can demand appropriations from the town which, generally speaking, the town may not reject. And the School Department spent far more money than any other town agency; teachers salaries *alone* in the fiscal year, 1956, took $1,313,639 out of total town expenditures of $8,534,624.

Second, a substantial increase took place in assessments upon the town of Watertown from the county and from metropolitan agencies. Under Massachusetts law and practice, neither Middlesex County, the Metropolitan District Commission (a significant provider of services, sewers, and amenities) or the Metropolitan Transportation Agency, had material taxing authority of their own: they assess towns and cities, within the areas which then must raise the money. In fact, increased assessments (or *anticipated* increases in assessments) from all three of these autonomous units of government explained a substantially larger proportion of the tax hike than did the salary raises. The amateurishness with which the whole contest was conducted is shown by the fact that there was little discussion of these costs during the entire affair; yet clearly, if one is concerned with democratic control and so on, the Metropolitan District Commission was far less subject to any effective control by anybody than the town employees—in addition to the fact that these agencies did far more to raise the tax rate! It would seem, as pointed out above, that the town insiders could have made a very strong case for themselves by agreeing that the tax rate was far too high, *but* blaming it (correctly enough for purposes of political discussion) on these agencies. They could then have gone ahead and attacked the city of Boston which, in general, cast more votes *than all the suburbs put together* on MTA matters; then attacked the state for its appointments to the Metropolitan District Commission. Both agencies, although certainly performing valuable and needed services, could have been subject to criticism for indifference or at points substandard service to some suburbanites (indeed all transportation authorities are subject to such criticism). And finally the Watertown leaders could have, justly enough, criticized the county for wastefulness in expenditure of tax dollars (for many years, horrendous cases of such wastefulness kept being suggested). Along such lines, it would seem that the Watertown leaders could have constructed a coalition which would include most dissatisfied Watertowners, newcomers and insiders.

The fact that they did not do so, is, so far as I know, because it did not occur to them to do so. There was nothing in the nature of political ties between Watertown leaders and those in the City of Boston; the Mayor of Boston at the time had no particular following in Watertown and probably would not even have been widely known there. There was no strong representation of Watertown on the MDC, although there may have been some inhibiting factors there; the MDC might have cut down on some optional services, parks, tennis courts, etcetera, and some Watertowners were employed by the MDC. The people who ran county matters tended to be in Cambridge and Lowell and there was no suggestion of ties with Watertown. Massachusetts has not had at any time within the memory of man—certainly not since the Republican "escalator" disappeared in the late 30s—any political machine or organization crossing community boundaries, as Florida and Illinois clearly have had.

The real point was rather that, first, the town accounts and financial statements were not prepared in a way which made it at all easy to emphasize the costs of MDC, MTA, and the county. Of course, leaders with the kind of political ingenuity hypostatized above would have redesigned the town's financial statements so such contributions (assessments) stood out in bold relief. There is not, so far as I know, any comparative study of Massachusetts local financial statements and their implications politically; generally, in the 50s, they were not unusually revealing, chiefly because they were rather unimaginatively prepared. Since the MDC was, to most Watertowners and to most citizens of Greater Boston, despite its importance for them, hardly more than three initials, and since counties in Massachusetts are obscure and arcane entities, known only to the governmental groupie or political pro, few are aware of the agencies or their assessing authority. (Political scientists have long called the "county" "the dark continent of American government" but if this phrasing be accurate for counties in Illinois or Indiana, some much more dismissive phrase should be used about Massachusetts counties–something like "the invisible tracing on the wallpaper" of state government).

There was a third reason why prudent town officials had to budget for a higher tax rate at the time, but over which the town had no control at all. Massachusetts communities had long come to depend upon substantial transfers from the state in order to meet their expenses. State officials are, under the law, expected to distribute funds for several purposes to the towns and cities, on the basis of the state's receipts from taxation. These distributions are made, of course, after the fiscal year has started and after the town or city has actually spent a fair amount of money. But towns and cities can not very well change their tax rate in the middle of a fiscal year. So the state had for a number of years supplied estimates as to what it expected to be able to "return" to towns and cities, on the basis of estimates as to tax collections for the coming year. Such estimates, in the nature of the case, generally err on the side of caution; but, nevertheless, a town would be wildly irresponsible not to take them into account in doing its fiscal planning. In the year with which we were concerned, state financial officials expected a recession and therefore estimated towns and cities would receive somewhat less than they had been accustomed to expect. (It is also possible that some of the state financial officials who made these estimates had a certain bias in favor of estimating relatively low receipts in order to strengthen the movement which was then growing for a state-imposed sales tax; but this is simply an impressionistic guess).

8

The Homeowners and Tenants Protective Association

It should be stressed to those unfamiliar with local tax practices: the tax rate in Massachusetts, as in several other parts of the world, refers to the rate of taxation on real estate per $1,000 valuation. The $1,000 valuation is based upon the value of the given piece of property as specified by the assessors. Assessment of property values is by no means stable and consistent anywhere under any circumstances; and it was probably more difficult to reach an agreed-upon valuation in Massachusetts towns in the 50s than in most of the world.

Although there was considerable retail and some manufacturing property in Watertown, the bulk of the town was, of course, residential. So, the tax base was chiefly on homes and housing. The new people who moved into town between 1946 and 1953 had, in any case, been hit in many instances by an unanticipated increase in the rate of tax on their property for this reason: in Watertown, as in many other towns, so long as houses remained in the same family, at least if the family was actually living in Watertown, changes in the assessed value of the property tended to be marginal and incremental. However, when houses were acquired by somebody from outside Watertown, the assessors tended to jump the assessment; often, to be sure, simply to take into account the fact that property often changed hands at a price way above the previous assessed value. But to people like the newcomers to Watertown described above, to whom a house of their own was a genuinely big commitment, such a jump would often constitute an unexpected wallop. In a good many cases, it is reasonable to presume that neither the seller nor the real estate agent had warned them to expect it; on the contrary, the preexisting valuation was probably cited to them, if they asked.

It is also likely and indeed certain that a number of these newcomers were suffering their economic hurts because of their investment in a house. On the whole, they tended to be people to whom the purchase of a house would not be regarded by a cold-blooded financial analyst as necessarily worth the burden and risk. In the nature of the case, people in this sort of income level are likely to make the house purchase decision when near the top of their economic benefits receipt for any given cycle. Such factors as children growing older would certainly make some of them less well-off a few years later. And, as pointed out above, in the area, there was an expected and to be sure noticeable recession at the time of the big tax rate jump—which almost certainly meant that people lost overtime, higher commissions, and so on. And, just like the town employees, many of the new homeowners would be aware of the inflation of 1950–53, because in their case, due to the recession, they could not play catch-up in 1956.

The Movement

So a citizen's movement sprang up in opposition to the tax increase and what was blamed for it, the pay raises. It called itself the Homeowners and Tenants Protective Association. (Tenants were affected over time because tax raises would lead to rent increases). In fact, there seem to have been, as one would expect, a vast preponderance of homeowners in the movement, rather than tenants.

The town meeting members and the town employees referred to all of them as "new" people—new to Watertown. Most of them were. But a few were "new" people only in the sense that they did not "know" Watertown, had never been visible in town affairs.

Even the leaders of the movement, those who formed it, were new to each other. They said, "In the beginning we were three. That is as near as we can get to it now. . .We were introduced by a mutual friend." (The only point in any of the interviewing where informants were unwilling to give details was the name of this friend. I suspect that he was an active Republican, probably living in Watertown, though perhaps active only in state politics, not in local politics. Two alternative reasons may be given for his bringing the three men together: on the one hand, he may have thought that fighting the tax rise could serve to hurt the Democrats, who held most offices, in the town. If so, he was mistaken; for in the event, no prominent Republican took the side of the Homeowners, and most of them supported the town employees. I would guess this man was among those who supported the employees, ultimately. But, on the other hand, the three men might well be perceived by a person established in party affairs in a moderate state and a moderate community as a threat; by temperament, they were the kind of men who, eight years later, going along with Goldwater in Massachusetts, with vigor and zeal, embarrassed many established Republicans. It is easy to imagine an established Republican leader trying to head such potential zealots, such conceivable "Young Turks," in a direction which would not embarrass the set of leaders to which he belonged).

They continued, "the night the three of us met we had the idea we'd start the snowball rolling so it might become a snowstorm." Note the contrast with the town meeting members who constituted a set of people with scores of crisscrossing networks of relationships, built up over the years, through kin and church and recreation as well as employment and/or politics.

Those with active experience in political campaigns know that at the headquarters of such campaigns, during the duration, intense relationships develop as no doubt they do also in military campaigns. "We hustled things through very rapidly. None of us really knew each other to start with, but by the time we'd been working together a few weeks, we were old buddies!"

This set of three men said that they "planned a referendum at the very first meeting between the three of us. That was the purpose of our organization. We worked with each other to get money, our first $100.00." (this figure, to be taken quite seriously, shows among other things how little they had in the way of initial resources or contacts. Note that the idea of a referendum was almost certainly borrowed from Miles Robinson in the events of a few years back, reported above; it is unlikely it would have occurred to these men otherwise.)

"We got supporters while raising money. At the beginning we were threatened with vague harassments." This may have been true; but if so, they were almost certainly, in the Watertown political climate, very vague.[37] More likely, the men simply felt what many people in our society do when they challenge authority or its minions. "It was a pretty daring fellow who'd let his name be used" in support of the movement at the beginning—although many people, they said, gave money ($1 or $2) without letting their names be used. "We were certainly a grass roots movement. Everybody who was a town leader opposed us. We wanted to get town leaders, because we were mostly a bunch of greenhorns, but except for Robinson, Gregory, and Lightbody, we never did." It is probably that, bearing in mind the people they could appeal to most, they might have weakened rather than strengthened the movement by getting town leaders on their side. At that time, and on a continuing basis, many people in Massachusetts tended to take the position that leaders as such were suspect. A few years later, John Collins beat John Powers for Mayor of Boston, probably in part because the latter had endorsements from absolutely everybody who was anybody in any kind of civic or political activity.

Of course a few town figures, defeated in the 1953 battle, came out on the Homeowner's side. The most important of these was Miles Robinson (see above). According to a town official, "These Homeowners were a new group. . .They were looked down on by old line Democrats *and* Republicans as radical and rabid. . .Finally, the Homeowners did get Miles Robinson in it. My father and Miles' father fought each other most of their lives—and I've fought with Miles—but he made a difference. When they got Miles, they got a fine old line family who covered up the fact that they are not in good repute. They are not the kind of people who know how to run Watertown."

The Homeowners campaign had, almost of necessity, for lack of funds, to be run as it was, on a neighborhood, coffee-party basis. One family would invite in a group of neighbors to have the issues explained. Incidentally, I suspect that—since this happened on a more intense scale than anything else of the sort, at least in the post-war years, in Watertown—quite aside from its effect on the campaign, the neighborhood-style meetings did mildly increase the sense of neighborliness among newcomers to the town. There were also a considerable number of circulars and advertisements. Two points were hammered at: (1) the tremendous hike in the tax rate and (2) the fact that such a large proportion of town meeting members were town employees.

As pointed out above, the hike in the tax rate argument was essentially invalid and after a while some of the leadership of the Homeowners equivocated on this. One of the few people in town who understood intellectually the nature of town finances, without having any connection with town government or town officials, was told that if she signed the petition it would "save $10 on your tax rate." The canvasser who told her this was the wife of a prominent Homeowner. The woman being canvassed retorted (she said): "You know that isn't so. Let me see your husband before I sign it." When she did, the husband according to her admitted "Yes, I know that isn't so. But that's how we are going to get the vote."

The Homeowners made a good deal of the other point, too, of course, town meeting members being town employees. Reported one: "I not only told everybody in our precinct that 18 of the 27 town meeting members were town employees, but that, of course Maurice Sheehan is in the Fire Department *and* Chairman of the Housing Authority and that nine of the twenty-seven town meeting members from our precinct live in the Housing Authority project and don't pay any taxes themselves. . ." (Property taxes are imposed, of course, only on owners of property).

During the course of the campaign, since the tax hike argument was being rebutted, Homeowners came to emphasize more the town meeting member point. Town meeting members, it was aggressively maintained, must not be permitted to rule town meeting in their own interests.

There are so many ironies in this case that at one time I toyed with the idea of calling it *Irony in Watertown.* But one of the delicious ironies is that, having started out in reaction to a tax hike, Homeowners leaders found that the argument was invalid. So they shifted to the ground of principle: town meeting members should not be town employees. However, they did not (except in such irresponsible, gossipy, and exaggerated stories as that about Sheehan and the Housing Authority) show how, in fact, town meeting members were "ruling in their own interest." But nevertheless said one of them, speaking for several others, "We didn't go into this to make money. *Principle has no price.* The ones I worked with felt the same way; they got kind of mad. $5 (tax hike in 1955) and another $10 in 1956 and yet no improvement in the town facilities, and town employees are at the top salarywise." Factually, this was wrong. There *were* on-going improvements in town facilities, in the Fire Department, in recreation, in the library, for instance. There is no record of the salaries of Homeowners as compared with those of town employees, the latter may have been higher; but town employees were paid a bit less than people with similar skills in town employment in several adjoining and near-by towns and cities, Winchester, Waltham, Newton, notably.

9

The Counter-Movement

Naturally, town employees and their supporters mounted a counter-movement. All full-time employees were "assessed" to support it; and it would have been a brave employee who, without good reason, did not pay his assessment. As one of the leaders of this organization said, "We organized our effort like any political campaign." Only it was more businesslike than the characteristic Watertown political campaign.

One objective of a political campaign is, of course, to discourage your opponent's supporters. In order to do this, the Committee distributed a dittoed list of those who had signed the petition for a referendum. Prominent figures in town, *and those who sold supplies or services to the town or to town employees,* had their name placed in capitals. According to the Homeowners (not confirmed by the Citizens) the list was divided up among different departments, for the purpose of effective harassment. It is reasonable to suppose, however, that from the standpoint of the Citizens this was simply an effort to identify people who "needed to be straightened out;" but, naturally enough, when a filling-station proprietor or a barber, serving a number of town employees, requested that their names be withdrawn from the referendum petition, the Homeowners regarded this as proving harassment.

But according to some informants (who alleged they shifted entirely towards favoring the town employees for this reason) the Homeowners gave as bad as they got. "There was" I was told, "this poor fellow at the postoffice (a town meeting member and a federal employee). . .his 'Yes' vote supporting the town employees almost ruined him. The Homeowners accused him of deliberately destroying the mail, provoked an investigation (which led to his suspension), etc."

The Homeowners were also said by town employees to harass them both at home and work with anonymous, insulting phone calls.

10

Bitterness of the Conflict

The Homeowners' advertising addressed the Citizens Committee: "For what purposes are town employees Town Meeting Members? Is it not to vote higher salaries for themselves and their friends? . . . You evidently think it right for a selfish group to control the governing body of Watertown? Is this what you mean by 'preservation of the town meeting form of government?'" The Citizens Committee counter-attacked by accusing the Homeowners of using the Big Lie technique of political campaigning.

A good deal of personal acrimony and bitterness occurred. A prominent middle-aged town personality said "Nothing like this ever happened before in Watertown. This was dreadful, dreadful, dreadful. It broke up families, ruined friendly relationships. Now, if I were to go downtown and be seen talking to people on the other side, my friends would soon hear all about it and want to know why—and it was true the other way around, too." When I asked another town figure whether fights of this sort didn't happen in a lot of towns, he replied, "Well, I heard of a town in California that had a fight similar to ours, but I haven't heard of anything around here that was anywhere near as bitter."

The Homeowners were accused (probably correctly) by a good many town workers of adopting the attitude "you're just our employees." (This attitude would have been more familiar to town employees in sections of Belmont, Winchester, Wellesley, Dover, and other suburbs with a higher proportion of wealthy or professional people—but in Watertown it had not been so common at this time.) Reported one department officer, "Calls kept coming in to the department heads saying 'Men are loafing; men are loafing.' In one case it was a man standing over an open manhole to make sure nobody tumbled in. And another case: For years when a dump truck goes to the dump, the men who are not driving stand and wait in the neighborhood where they've been picking up. This is because one man can handle everything to and at the dump, and if the others are on the truck and it is in an accident, they (in effect, though oversimplified, the insurers) may add an extra charge to the disability system. So, these Homeowners complain to the head of the Highway Department. He orders the men, then, to go to the dump with the driver, and the Chairman of the Retirement System sees red, because it adds to the potential liability of the system."

"And still another time a big complaint came in that a lot of town employees were lying down on the highway, for Heaven's sake! Well, first, what these men were doing was sniffing along the highway, trying to locate a gas leak. And, second, they weren't town employees at all. They worked for the *gas* company!"

Another town employee said, "Some of these people cut quotations out of the paper and sent them to us. I've saved a whole stack of insulting anonymous cards from them. And almost two years later I got a card with some item from Milwaukee about a fireman out there who had done something wrong, and the note said 'All you guys are doing something wrong!'"

It was said that employees who applied for early retirement at this time were motivated by a feeling of disgust. "Before there used to be a certain amount of satisfaction in working for the town. Now, there is not."

The Homeowners, on the other hand, felt that they were being harassed by town employees. To anyone familiar with what happened to those who fought city hall or the county courthouse in Kansas City under Pendergast or in rural Florida or mountain Tennessee or in Texas or a good many other places, there is quaintness about their complaints. Most of the world should have it so good! But, looking at it another way, the mere fact that matters of this sort evoked a feeling of being treated with profound injustice reveals a good deal about the gentleness of political in-fighting in Watertown and presumably, since there was no sense of Watertown being different, in the adjoining suburbs. It was funny, to anyone who knew something of these other parts of the world, to take part in the following colloquy. Several of the prominent Homeowners were telling me how badly they were now treated by the town employees. Their repeated remarks were all general; I pressed them for specifics. Finally, they came up with what might have been described in some circles as a dilly: It seems that Watertown police had generally helped Watertown drivers who got into minor trouble (parking or speeding tickets) with the police of the larger community in which most Watertowners have occassion to drive, Cambridge. The Cambridge police, if asked it by the Watertown police, would forget or quash a charge. But now, it was pointed out to me with indignant force, if a Homeowners member asked the Watertown police to fix a a Cambridge parking ticket for him, nothing would happen. This was harassment!

Nevertheless, such a thing is resented; when people have taken away from them favors which they have come to expect, they feel discriminated against. Some of the other acts of "harassment" as felt by the Homeowners were probably regarded by the town employees as natural political horse-play in the old Watertown tradition–but the Homeowners did not "know Watertown" and that tradition. The visit of nine inspectors in one day (none of them asked for) at Miles Robinson's house, or the repeated unnecessary rattling of garbage cans outside Homeowners houses early in the morning . . . have already been mentioned. However, this latter may well have been due only to expectation and attention; although in no way was I involved in any conflict with anybody in town or with the sanitation company which collected trash in Belmont, where I lived, I did notice a lot more rattling of cans, for several weeks after I heard this story–because the story had sensitized me to that noise.

One event was clearly meant as a joke, but was not so taken by the Homeowners. No-parking regulations were assiduously enforced in those streets where a lot of Homeowners lived, against *their* cars, although this has never previously been done. In answer to a complaint about this, a policeman engaged in ticketing apparently said, "You know what a police force is for—to protect people against robbery. I'm protecting us against robbery by you. You're robbing us of our raises!"

A Homeowner leader alleged: "A great deal was done though children. Children of town employees would call Homeowners children names and make it unpleasant. When Mr. Robinson suggested that this harassment of children be investigated, there was a story about it in the papers. So, then, the Assistant Superintendent of Schools called a meeting and said that (Robinson's statement) constituted a campaign against town employees!"

11

The Referendum

"Despite the heat and a violent thunderstorm," (according to the *Watertown Press*) and despite the fact that the polls were only open six hours for the special referendum on June 13, 1956, over 10,000 voters turned out to cast their ballots on it. This was roughly 54 percent of those eligible to vote; in comparison only 9,782 votes had been cast in the regular March town-election of 1955, and a mere 1,405 persons had voted for delegates to the national Presidential conventions in April, 1956 (to be sure, there was no contest on the Republican side for President in 1956 and Massachusetts was not a focal state for Democratic contests). In the 1956, 1957, and 1958 annual town elections, however, over 12,000 persons cast ballots, presumably because of the stirred-up interest in town matters. And, it should be noted that in the general fall elections of November, 1956, when the Presidency and all six state constitutional officers (as well as county officers and state legislators) were voted on, 20,165 persons in Watertown cast ballots. In other words, although the referendum issue seemed vital to some, a good many people were not moved to come to the polls, presumably because it did not interest or excite them much.

One reason, no doubt, why the vote was as low as it was, was that there were seventeen questions, technically separate, to be voted on; in essence they were all the same: *Shall the pay raises as approved by the town meeting be maintained or not?* But since the pay raises and related matters appeared in a number of different articles of the warrant, the referendum had to have a separate question on each one of these articles.

According to the *Watertown Press*'s calculations, an average of the votes on all seventeen questions showed that 3,514 supported the limited town meeting, 5,895 opposed it. The town employees were beaten 12 to 7.

Or, so it seemed. Nevertheless, the same week, the town officials notified the electorate that the tax rate would still be set at $16.80. The day *after* the referendum election the State Department of Taxation, which, under the law, must approve all local tax rates, approved the Watertown rate as previously set by the town authorities. The reason for maintaining the $61.80 rate was that the Homeowners had failed to provide for cutting out Article 3 of the Warrant, which contained the appropriations figures for the year. And the appropriations figures were calculated on the assumption that the pay raises, etc., would go through.

The Selectmen then announced that they intended to pay the new rates of pay, regardless of the referendum. Although the new rates of pay were set in Articles 13 through 30 of the warrant, which the electorate had voted to rescind, the actual appropriation of money for the salaries was, said the Selectmen, contained in Article 3, the appropriations article, and they intended to be guided by that. In a public announcement, the Selectmen said, "Because of error or lack of knowledge, the leaders of the petitioners failed to include Article 3 in the petition. Thus the voters at large of the town were deprived by the failure of the petitioners of the opportunity to pass fully and effectively on these matters. . ."

This was, the Selectmen claimed, entirely the Homeowner's fault. "Prior to the last day for withdrawing the petition, the leaders of the petition and their attorney met with the Selectmen, Town Clerk, Auditor, Town Counsel, and were advised that the petition, because of its failure to include Article 3, could not accomplish its purpose. . .and that a vote of the voters at large could not change (the fact that in the opinion of the town officers employees will still receive the raise granted by the limited town meeting). . .These matters will be argued pro and con until ultimately some time from now determined by the courts. We believe the following to be the proper course.

We recommend that necessary steps be taken to bring this matter before a Special (limited) Town Meeting (and) that the Advisory Board of Review, the Finance Committee, and the (Limited) Town Meeting reaffirm (the raises). . .

"We further recommend that the voters of Watertown at large accept such action and place their confidence in the duly appointed Board of Review, Finance Committee, and duly elected Town Meeting Members who, in the opinion of Town Counsel have properly, legally, *and finally* (italics mine, L.A.D.) appropriated funds now due town employees at the rates appropriated. . .Conclusion: Effective this week, ending June 27, 1956, town employees will receive the weekly pay (raises) voted to them at the Annual Town Meeting of 1956." Andrew Jackson, reportedly, said in relation to the Supreme Court opinion in the Cherokee cases: "John Marshall has made his decision; now let him enforce it." So, similarly, the Selectmen of Watertown to the voters of that town.

The Homeowners had a natural and logical counter. They proposed in an open letter that an excess account be set up for the funds appropriated for pay raises, and that "this amount be returned to taxpayers in next year's levy." That is, they accepted the tax rate of $61.80 as final for that fiscal year, but proposed that the following year's taxes be reduced by the amount attributable to the pay raises, and that no raises actually be paid; so that presumably the tax rate for the following fiscal year could be lowered, from the monies thus set aside.

At this point, the Treasurer, a Republican and an Armenian (whereas most of the town officers were Democrats and Irish), stepped in. His office, in fact, issued checks and made disbursements. He declared that he would recognize the results of the referendum, and he added that due to the uncertainty of the whole situation, he could not now continue to pay the cost-of-living bonus which the town employees had been receiving for several years. So, instead of getting a 6 percent pay hike, they would face in practice, at least for the time being, a reduction of almost 12 percent. According to one informant at Town Hall, "The Selectmen went around and ordered the Department Heads to prepare the higher payrolls (including the 12 percent and the 6 percent and submit them. The Treasurer followed a Selectman around from office to office countermanding the

Selectman's order. The Selectman then ordered the Department heads to follow his order or he would bring them up on charges. . .Actually, the Auditor prepared two warrants (on the basis of which the Treasurer made disbursements)–one for the higher and one for the lower rate of pay–and wrote across the higher that he could not sign it. . ."

Some town employees, finding themselves unexpectedly deprived of about 12 percent of their anticipated wages, were forced to borrow money; they resented this.

A two hour meeting, on the 28th of June, between the Selectmen and the Town Counsel, on the one hand, and representatives of the Homeowners on the other was described by the *Watertown Press* as "rowdy and argumentative." Discussion ranged, said the *Press,* "from the most technical legal points to complaints over alleged abuse by town employees of those voting against the pay hike."

The major legal argument was over Article 3: the Homeowners pointed out that they, in their judgment, could not have moved to reverse Article 3, because then *all* appropriations for the town would have been invalidated, and town government would have stopped. But the Selectmen and Counsel argued that, since the referendum procedure did not provide for splitting an article or modifying it, this was the only option open to the Homeowners. In fact, if all appropriations had been cut out, presumably the School and Health Departments would have shortly ceased to operate, and the State, in its capacity as protector of the public, would have stepped in and operated the town. The State does this when a municipality is, for instance, bankrupt (as New Bedford was at one time),[38] and a town that did not make any appropriations would be like a bankrupt. The real point was that the 1919 statute under which Watertown was governed was not clear on the nature of a referendum. The Homeowners naturally burst into laughter when one of the Selectmen pointed out (correctly enough) that Watertown "does not operate under the standard form of town meeting." They were less amused when another Selectman said "the people were becoming a bunch of rabble rousers." In the chaste understatement of the *Watertown Press*, this remark "roused the ire of some ladies present and brought the meeting to a close."

12

Reconsideration of Sorts

The Homeowners now made the proposal that instead of the wage raise, the fluctuating cost-of-living allowance should be reinstated. According to calculations by the Finance Committee, based upon the official cost-of-living index, inflation over the preceding base period had been great enough by now so that, in fact, town employees would receive 17 percent over their base pay on a cost-of-living allowance calculation, as compared with the slightly over 18 percent they would receive under the wage hike approved by the town meeting. Obviously, the slight differences involved could have no material effect on the current tax rate; but for older employees approaching retirement, the substantial difference in the retirement basis on which pensions would be calculated was a matter of moment. In fact, if, as seemed quite plausible, inflation during the next year or two kept up at the same rate, the tax rate would become higher with the Homeowners plan than with that of the limited town meeting! Instead of saving $10 on the tax rate, the Homeowners might easily add a $1.50 or so to it, one of the numerous ironies of the situation!

A Special Town meeting, as recommended by the Selectmen, took place on August 6. Pro forma, the whole set of recommendations, already approved, were reviewed again by the Finance Committee and the Advisory Board of Review, and again approved. The Homeowners alternate plan for restoring the "fluctuating" cost-of-living allowance had also been placed on the warrant. However, the Advisory Board, for some reason, had not bothered to consider the matter. Again, the Homeowners were faced with a technical block. Miles Robinson, as President, now, of the Homeowners, argued that, since the article was in the warrant, it should have been considered by the Advisory Board; but the Chairman of that Board said he had "never received a request" to consider it, and Town Counsel ruled that anybody who places an item on the agenda, "has the responsibility of following through and seeing that the proposed amendment was actually considered by the Advisory Board."

Once again, the argument centered on what appeared to the naive democrats of the Homeowner group to be completely technical issues, rather than substantive ones. One gets the impression of the Homeowners protesting furiously but rather blindly against people who speak another, legalistic, often jargon-filled language. Said a prominent Homeowner, for instance: "It was clever to wait until the last minute. *You* (the *Selectman and Advisory Board*) *should have shown some understanding and friendship.*" (Italics mine, LAD.) This, on the floor of the town meeting, to which the Chairman of the Advisory Board replied, "It is the law and we have no control over it." But if the law is a master, and not a servant of good will, is it not an ass? Most likely seventy-five or eighty years previously when the Irish-Americans first began to press demands upon the Yankee-run town of those days, the old Yankees used similar "tricks" to keep them from being heard, heeded, or effective. But the Irish-Americans in Watertown, as in many other communities, had cultural capacity for handling this sort of political legalism, and, if not in the beginning, soon thereafter gave as good as they got—turning the contests into supposedly fun-filled battles as suggested above. The Homeowners were not prepared for such a game. Parliamentary technique was not a game to them, and of course it was not to some of the town employees either, who were suffering from unpaid bills or worrying about pensions. But, basically, we have two different conceptions: one, the town meeting as a forum, open to all (the theory of the fundamental statute), and two, the town meeting as an arena for parliamentary stratagems: "may the best man win and the devil take the hindmost."

13

What Is the Town Meeting Anyhow? Or Where?

By now, the focus of the issue had completely shifted. The tax rate could not be, everybody tacitly agreed, affected much either way—the difference in dollars was too slight between the two plans. Of prime interest, now, was the location of sovereignty. Who by right should make decisions and how? At the August meeting, the Town Counsel was asked if the referendum of June was in any way binding on the town. He replied, "The town meeting can not be limited by the referendum. It can take action as it sees fit. It can vote, as it did in the spring, and if there are objections, there can be another referendum." Presumably, and so on, *ad infinitum.* Of course, his opinion rested on the real ambiguities of the basic statute: who was the town meeting, anyway? One can understand the compromise which the drafters of that statute made; it was unfortunate for the town that during the intervening years, when nobody used the referendum procedure, somebody did not clarify the code, so as to avoid precisely this sort of conflict. But, as it was, no one could then say the Town Counsel was wrong *or* that the Homeowners were wrong on the issue of law—nobody knew what the statute meant.

Naturally, the August town meeting confirmed its decision of the spring and overruled the referendum. Reported the *Watertown Press:* "At a turbulent four-hour session. . .before a near capacity crowd, (they) voted to restore the salary plan, voted at the last March meeting. The key vote was 179 to 63," with about eighty members absent or not voting. Following the meeting, according to the *Press,* "people gathered in knots outside the building and an argument between two groups of women was broken up by Lt. Flaherty who urged all to go home quietly."

A New Referendum? Appeal to the Courts

So, the Homeowners, again naturally, petitioned for a new referendum which, they insisted, should ensure that "representatives of town meeting must conform to the will of the citizens." The Selectman pointed out that, by this time, the practical dollars and cents difference between the Homeowners somewhat modified fluctuating cost-of-living plan and the salary plan would be very slight, and added in a public statement: "What then are these. . .so-called (Homeowners) leaders seeking to accomplish? Confusion, dissension, loss of morale, retardation of the good conduct of the town's affairs, the spending of a substantial sum of town money for extra meetings and elections, these have been the result (of their actions)." (*Watertown Press,* August 16, 1956). (It is worthy of comment that although the state election campaign was well under way at that time, and although the Selectmen, at least, were actively involved in some aspects of it, there is no record that anybody related these town conflicts in anyway to campaigns for state office).

By this time, the town employees had secured a new and very experienced counsel, long associated with the association of police in the Commonwealth, George V. McLaughlin, Sr. He made the point that since police, fire, and health are matters of public concern, vital to the State as a whole, salaries of officials in these departments are not referendable. What he said was that *these items are too important to be left to the judgment of the citizenry at any given town.* After mulling over this argument, the Selectmen announced that they would not now accept the petition for a referendum, because police, fire, and health salaries ought not, as a matter of right, to be referendable. "We therefore state, on advice of counsel, that we will deny the petition for a referendum as filed." The Homeowners had two options then: to modify their petition to apply only to the "nonvital" town employees (in the library or recreation departments, presumably, for instance) or to appeal to the courts.

They chose the latter alternative. They asked the Superior Court for a writ, ordering the holding of a second referendum election, on the basis of the petition as filed. A meeting was held in order to try to reach a compromise between the Town employees and the Homeowners, to avoid court action, but it broke up in disagreement.

The town employees had already filed what amounted to a countersuit against the Treasurer, requesting that he be ordered to pay out to them the 12 percent cost-of-living allotment, which was being held up all this time—of course held in reserve.

Both suits were decided by Judge Swift of the Superior Court on October 16, 1956. First, the Treasurer was ordered to pay all town employees at the higher rate of pay voted by the town meeting in the spring. Second, the Court found that since "many of these subjects (in municipal government) require intensive study, discussion, *and possible compromise* (italics mine, L.A.D.). . .to arrive at definite and correct results. . .it is fair to assume and I so find that the questions involved in the classification of employees and. . .salaries for employees are so intricate and cover such a vast field that the best interests of the municipality would be met by having this study of these intricate questions made by representatives of the people in the form of a limited town government. Careful and judicious consideration of the matters involved could not be given in referendum meeting as would be possible in a limited town meeting." So he denied the Homeowners petition for another referendum, and interpreted the previous referendum as purely advisory.

His reasoning may, from an empirical standpoint seem valid; but it is hard to justify general town meetings under it, bearing in mind the empirically demonstrable fact that most voters do not attend most meetings; and that a crowd gathers, and overrules the established committees, only on some matter of public excitement such as police salaries.[39] The Judge, of course, did not address himself to any such matter.

Judge Swift also pointed out that if salaries of town employees were regarded as issues which could be changed by referendum and several referenda were in fact called, "constant confusion. . .would be the inevitable result and the municipality would fail to succeed in carrying out the purposes for which it was established." But what about several town meetings in one year?

The Homeowners appealed to a higher court, and in December, 1957, fourteen months later, the State Supreme Court reversed Judge Swift's decision; it was willing evidently to risk "constant confusion" and lack of judicious consideration. By this time, of course, the salary issue was a completely dead one; the employees, due to inflation, ironically would have been getting more under the Homeowner's cost-of-living allowance than under the town meeting wage hike. The Supreme Court's reasoning was that (as pointed out earlier in this paper) the words "town meeting" were used in different ways in the basic statute and that the intent of the legislature forty years previously was that such matters as compensation plans should be matters which could be changed by referendum. The Selectmen were then ordered to hold a referendum, of the sort refused in 1956, not later than the annual town meeting of 1958, in March.

14

A Second Referendum: Anti-Climatic

Since the town employees would have been getting more money (because of a further rise in the cost-of-living indices used as a base) under the Homeowners cost-of-living plan than under the wage hike, the second referendum, held on February 24, 1958, just before the annual town meeting, was an anti-climax! Indeed, the Homeowners as an organization took no stand on the second referendum. They abandoned their own baby. The general confusion and lack of interest meant that no significant attention was paid to the matter and there was a very small vote. As the policemen and firemen had predicted, back in 1953, a small vote generally meant support for town employees (because they and their kin are more certain to vote than most other people). The pay scale plan, under which the employees had been paid anyway for almost two years, was approved.

For the time being the issue about wage hikes and tax rates stopped being the subject of passionate contention. A few years later, other conflicts about payments of town employees and the like again came into controversy. This number of elected town meeting members was cut approximately in half by a decision of the town as a whole, making running the limited town meeting less unwieldy. And in the 1970s various changes in the Watertown form of government were made which some outside observers describe as drastic. But the particular episode with which this report is concerned was over. The fight about the locus of sovereignty and the nature of representative democracy would not be further illuminated by tracing the history of these later years.

Town Meetings and Time Consumption

It is, however, worth suggesting one further extremely significant point. The expectation that people shall take direct part in their own governance, whether in church or town, does have under modern conditions an effect. That effect is this: there is much greater likelihood of relatively marginal issues arousing great passion and excitement. Any one who has had contact with a number of Unitarian and Congregational churches, the churches which grew out of the Massachusetts established state church, and has had occasion to compare them with Methodist or Roman Catholic churches will be impressed by the greater frequency of bitter factional conflict, sometimes centered on quite a minor matter, sometimes delaying for months the calling of a new minister (because there is no Bishop to handle the matter as among the Methodists or Roman Catholics). So, also, in Massachusetts towns. Also sheer amount of time, if it were ever calculated, spent by competent and worthy people in combats about minor matters of town and parish government must be enormous—and much greater than the amount of time regularly expended on such issues in other systems of governance, ecclesiastical and secular. Analogically, in these days of faculty participation in many universities, faculty members spend far more time on all sorts of matters than they used to when a President often controlled, with the assistance and help of a few senior faculty and Chairmen.

It is often argued, perhaps correctly, that the kind of local democracy and congregational control characteristic of Massachusetts permits the avoidance of severe trouble and conflict. This may be so. But the cost is surely considerable, as this case in a small way exemplifies. It is unlikely in a Southern county or a British or Scots borough that as much effort, passion, and ill-will would have gone into a matter of this sort. Of course, we are here speaking of statistical probabilities, not certainties. More exactly put, it is unlikely that as much effort, passion, and ill-will would have gone into such a matter, unless the underlying issues, economically or psychologically, mattered more to the participants. The Massachusetts system tends to make really sore issues out of what elsewhere would be minor conflict, which neither proves nor disproves its capacity to provide ways of resolving what would elsewhere be major issues.

The town meeting system also, whatever its merits, on average means more uncertainty and worry by town employees over wages, or so it is reasonable to infer. (See footnote 39 about police salaries in town politics). If estimates of the value of the time "expended" by town employees and prominent citizens on local conflicts were available for such towns as Watertown, Dracut (which underwent a bitter fight about certain town wages a few years later, which fight was resolved however by the State Labor Relations Board, rather than the courts), Wellesley, and Orleans, these being sociologically representative of four different types of towns, it would over a decade amount to a massive figure. The same massiveness of time spent in terms of value is presumably also present where faculties govern, rather than Presidents, and congregations rather than Bishops. Of course, in some instances—as in the England of the 1600–1620 period, out of which congregational systems of church government originated, and the town meeting, too—congregations will not be governed by bishops, and insist on governing themselves. But the question for consideration is: in constitutional revision and change, such as has taken place in many New England towns and in many congregational-type churches, either stealthily or openly, how much value should be attached to the town meeting open participation notion? or to full congregational participation? It should not be forgotten that when the Massachusetts Bay Colony adopted these devices, it was far more hierarchical sociologically, and there were far fewer people, than is now the case.

15

The Homeowners Resort to Genealogical Politics

The Homeowners, by the time of the final decision by the State Supreme Court in their favor, had ironically from a practical standpoint lost their major issue. It was clear to everyone, including themselves, that their proposals would not lower the tax rate. But the issue of "principle" which they had discovered remained. Town meeting members were, disproportionately, related to town employees, or were themselves town employees. In 1957 Homeowners had endorsed a slate of candidates for town meeting member on a genealogical criterion, that criterion being lack of relationship to any town meeting member. Seventy-seven of 106 candidates so endorsed won. In that year, no significant pay raise issue was voted on by town meeting.

Again, in 1958, Homeowners endorsed candidates for town meeting on a genealogical criterion. They stated they had won at least 50, and possibly 60, seats (they had not done enough research in a few cases to determine who was related to whom). However, it turned out that some of their endorsed candidates were, for example, members of the League of Women Voters who thought town employees were not paid enough. The Homeowners pressed for some changes in procedure at the annual meeting in 1958; despite their "victories" in the preceding elections, they were not much heeded on these matters. And when, to take further account of the continuing rise in the cost of living, a pay hike of $200 was voted for all town employees, a prominent Homeowner asked reconsideration of that proposal. The meeting voted 194 to 31 to sustain the rise (22 abstaining, about 70 absent).

16

Further Reflections on the Episode

How much difference did the whole episode make? Probably the cutting down of the size of the town meeting a few years later was influenced by the events of this period; but it may well have taken place anyway. Conceivably, the adoption of the entire state constitutional amendment and statute of standard procedures for representative town meetings, a few years later, may have owed a small bit to people's observations of this fight in Watertown. But, again, it represented a cleaning up, a recodification, which was likely to be attempted anyway.[40]

A few town employees may have retired prematurely. Working for the town became somewhat less enjoyable in some departments. But it is not likely that any one could trace out such effects with any specificity or accuracy.

One of the most important determinants of the defeat of the Homeowners was expressed by a reflective old Watertowner who had initially taken the side of Miles Robinson against the raise for police and fire, reported at the beginning of the story. But her position was perfectly consistent; she was against police and fire challenging the decisions of committees and town meeting, and later on she was in favor of accepting committee and town meeting recommendations for raises. Said she: "I own stock in a few companies. . .but people who are outside like me, the small stockholders, have no right to interfere. How can I know?. . .I can't even know the facts," She went ahead: "Many people who had put in thirty-five or forty years service (in the town meeting) voted for the raises just to vote against the Homeowners (and their claim that citizens should directly decide on such matters). You can't break down the structure of the established and proven government and of the people who've sat there (in town meeting) for forty years; and say 'they're crooks.' " I believe she spoke for many Republicans in town who, if the fight had been one of the old Yankee-Irish or Democrat-Republican fights might have opposed the town employees and the wage hikes, just to stir up the opposition. But the Homeowners challenged, not only the decision, but the system with its traditional moderateness; and so the kind of Republican whose preferred candidates were Leverett Saltonstall and Christian Herter at the state level, men of considerable moderateness and concern for stability, ultimately took the side of the Democratic town officials. Of course, Watertown did not have many of the gung-ho new-breed let's-get-back-to-basics-and-damn-the-implied-understandings Republicans who were more influential in Florida (for instance, around Orlando) or Arizona and who, a few years afterwards, nominated Barry Goldwater for President.

The position that this lady expressed was essentially that under the complicated conditions of modern life, it is downright irresponsible for the mass of voters to try to decide directly intricate matters normally considered by committee or by representatives. A few years later in quite a different context, the late Alice Bauer (Mrs. Raymond Bauer) discovered exactly the same attitude at work in Cambridge among a number of voters. In that city, as characteristically in Massachusetts, whether or not to fluoridate was decided by referendum; there were several referenda in Cambridge on fluoridation. She found out, to her and my surprise, that a good many persons who stated that they were against fluoridation and had voted or would vote against it in a referendum, nevertheless in a poll which she worked on, declared that public health experts should decide these matters–knowing that the experts would decide differently than they themselves. "We shouldn't be asked to decide" was a fairly frequent attitude in that poll.

Now, it is reasonable to suppose that such a response–relying on the experts when they hold attitudes opposed to one's own–will not be found where people distrust profoundly an entire system or establishement. It would have been quite unthinkable, for instance, that the radical Independentists in 1640, whether in Great Britain or New England, would feel that ultimate decisions of church and state should be left up to King and Bishops. It is not argued here that this reliance on experts or representative was the dominant one either in Watertown or Cambridge. But it was of some pertinence. It does, however, run counter to the various reports about "alienated" voters in Massachusetts which attained a certain fashionableness. It is quite possible, very simply, that some voters are alienated, others are not. But it is probable that some of the social scientists and journalists who detected alienation among voters probed in such a way as to bring it out, while failing to detect the attitude expressed by the lady just quoted, because it is not an attitude which they share, so far as public policies go. However, the self-effacing characteristics displayed in this attitude are desirable if local government is to work effectively without too much time being spent in controversy; a workable alternative, of course, is simple indifference to the issues of government, which also permits decisions to be made fairly expeditiously by those given a responsibility. This self-effacing attitude is particularly important where a referendum procedure is permitted; and it is of course a safeguard against volatile resort to non-cooperation, protests, demonstrations, and violence.

The Watertown episode, as pointed out in the introductory comments above, and in the concluding section below, had some of the characteristics which lead to fierce and violent opposition of doctrines and beliefs. But in fact it fizzled out, without much of a bang. One reason, and seemingly the most important, was that there would have been no hopeful way for the Homeowners, who essentially lost, even though they won a victory in Court, to resort to protests, demonstrations, and the like. Nevertheless, people have resorted to violence in the past when it would have seemed the odds were all against them; the organizers of Shay's Rebellion in Western Massachusetts in the 1780s or of the Whisky Rebellion in Western Pennsylvania in the 1790s might, one have thought, recognized the odds were all against them. The Whisky Rebellion, incidentally, was essentially a revolt against what were regarded as unfair taxes, imposed by an "establishment" in the nation's capitol, to its advantage, against something valued by those who rebelled. And some of the protests by Hispanic militants in the Southwest seem to have been equally unlikely to succeed.

But the Homeowners differed in several ways from these and other groups which have protested with some or considerable violence, even though the odds were all against them. The Homeowners did not share a common background and framework of shared experience to anywhere near the same extent as the rebels of Western Massachusetts (most of whom in the 1780s were farmers or in kindred occupations, who, in their localities, had known many of their fellowprotesters for years) in Shay's Rebellion, and unlike members of Hispanic protest groups in the Southwest. They were people, to be sure, drawn together by "mistreatment" and by a myth. But unlike many protest groups, they lacked multiplex ties binding them together. Consider the likely difference in the situation if the Homeowners had been members of both a religious and an ethnic minority, for example, if they had been black and Muslims, and confronted with the same situation. Possibly, even if they had simply, nearly all, belonged to the same trade and union, their resistance would have been more likely to continue; even if in that situation they might, in the United States of the 1950s have been more apt to resort to other political means than to violent protests.

In default of any such binding ties, it is not surprising that the Homeowner movement did not lead to any continuing difficulty for Watertown town government, and, insofar as it had an effect, was simply incorporated into town considerations about what it might be necessary to take into account. For such a movement to keep going, it needed to provide more rewards or stimuli or incentives than were available. What was there to induce agitative leaders to keep going in Watertown? The rewards were not great enough, nor was the scope of action ample enough to encourage them. Not surprisingly, a couple of years later, by chance as far as I was concerned, I encountered two of the prominent Homeowner leaders engaged in public activities, calling for some agitatorial talents, elsewhere in the Boston metropolitan region, not in Watertown. Presumably, the experience in Watertown had enhanced their taste for this sort of activity; but Watertown is far too much part of a larger complex for people with these skills to rest content on the whole with performing within the Watertown situation. Occasionally, as indicated in the introductory remarks above, it can be that a man of great natural ability, whose life has been spent in a town or city, will continue to work there, as a town official, even though there are greater opportunities elsewhere; the late J. Watson Flett, for many years the unquestioned leader in Belmont politics, was such a man (although even there in his later years, he was also appointed a Governor's Councillor to serve out an unexpired term). And although in a good many ways, for example as a leader among Armenian-Americans in general, he makes himself known beyond Watertown, apparently Treasurer Robert Hagopian was such a man in that community. But the Homeowners, by the nature of their recruitment process, would not be likely to have skillful leaders who had long-established ties to Watertown; the few old Watertowners whom they recruited were not likely to have been men who had established themselves as outstanding and the men who developed a skill in the kind of activity which running the Homeowners called for would, aside from anything else, have more fun and hope for more rewards by working in a movement of bigger scale, for example in the Goldwater effort, post–1962.

17

No Consultation With Experts Outside Watertown?

Since Watertown is very definitely part of a larger metropolitan region, part of a state government, it was surprising that so little use was made of resources—rich and readily available resources—outside Watertown. Boston College is a few minutes drive from Watertown Square; many Watertowners passed through Harvard Square every working day, most of them frequently. Boston College had at the time several scholars who knew about municipalities and their governance; Harvard University had people who knew a bit about local government at Littauer School (indeed, Miles Robinson's nephew-in-law had taught local government at Harvard a year or two previous to the episodes here reported and lived near-by in Weston). There were also exceptionally competent people in municipal research matters in a municipal research group concerned chiefly with Boston but with wide knowledge; the State maintained some experts in local affairs at the University of Massachusetts at Amherst. And several state departments had people who knew a good deal about the matters in dispute, or implied by the dispute: wage rates, comprative performance in various classes of jobs, and the like. Indeed, the state itself, and such municipalities as Salem, at the time, in order to avoid debate and ill feeling about how state and Salem employees were being paid, hired the personnel classification firm, Barrington Associates, to classify their employees. Yet none of these resources, so far as I know, were used; on the whole, no doubt, they would have supported the town employees against the Homeowners, but they would have added a good deal of credence and the appearance, at least, of objectivity to the town employees' demands and the town meeting's claims. And, presumably, the impact would not have all been one way. No one suggested consulting personnel classification firms (which, though expensive, would have been much less expensive than the costs of the fight). Some of the resentment and ill will of the Homeowners might have been lessened by the simple discovery that Watertown was not going above regional scales nor above the scale for similar suburbs in other big city metropoli; and had the town employees gone further, they probably could have shown that Watertown was getting better service for its dollars than a good many towns paying higher rates.

Why didn't anybody ask these sources? Why didn't anybody use them?[41]

18

And In Conclusion

Any reader of these pages who knows the story of how the taxpayers of Boston and Concord and Lexington and Watertown refused to pay the tax on tea, of how they stood up for the principle of representation against the British, must have been reminded of 1763–76. The Watertown town authorities resembled the British Cabinet of that time, the cabinet with which Edmund Burke so eloquently and ineffectively pleaded, in his famous Speech on Conciliation. The Watertown town officials, like the British statesmen of two centuries before, insisted on standing on legalisms; and they acted as though they thought a strategem for making a dependent look silly was as good a way of winning his support as treating him with "some understanding and friendship." Neither group, in any imaginative way, understood what was worrying the other side.

Yet, fundamentally, both the British cabinet and the Watertown town officials were right. Government has to be paid for; decisions have to be made in committee by established authorities. And yet established authorities who have no imagination, no sense of "understanding and friendship" are, as Burke so often and vainly said, jeopardizing their authority, losing the loyalty of those upon whom ultimately they must depend. Precisely because it is always more or less unpleasant to pay taxes, no government can afford totally to ignore the feelings of those who are taxed. Explanation, sympathy, understanding, are essential, when the taxpayers are capable of dealing with the tax-receivers on a more or less equal basis.

The issue was so terribly trivial; after all, very few people suffered much—just as, to look at facts squarely, hardly anybody in the Massachusetts Bay Colony suffered much from the tax on tea. But, the lack of sympathy, the ineptness, the stupidity in human terms, led to a tempest, in a teapot, shaking an Empire. Fortunately, for Watertown, and the world, no such dire consequences developed in this situation. But, although it is highly desirable that citizens learn that pure democracy, equal participation, etc., are myths in circumstances of the sort described, it is equally desirable that officials learn somehow to feel and express the "sympathy and understanding" for which in their better moments the Homeowners of Watertown were pleading.

Thinking about such issues as this in Watertown may be of use because, as Bird and Ryan point out in an extremely fascinating and well-written collection of reports about town squabbles in California, "The clash of interests in a town is as small as in the largest community. . .The conflicts are of the same essence as the issues that disrupt great societies. Man as a political animal is the same species whether functioning on a large scale or a small."[42] Studying the small-scale bitterness of Watertown may help suggest that the American Revolution, with all its attendant ill-will, may be judged at best in the same terms as a patriotic Watertowner used as she sadly looked at what had happened in her community: "I thought both sides were very wrong. . .but one side was worse wrong than the other."

Basically, it is probable that the British lost the Colonies because so many of the agents, colonial Governors, tax-collectors, etc., whom they sent to North America were arrogant, toplofty, unwilling to listen or to understand. In the little arena of Watertown, the amiable, pleasant, reasonably competent town officials who had run affairs moderately well for a quarter of a century or more were similarly unable or unwilling to see what it was that was bothering a substantial and vociferous part of the citizenry.

Substantive information would have been useful and desirable in the circumstances, as pointed out in the immediately preceding pages. When I first encountered the conflict, it was the complete inattention to this which shocked me most. And I am still shocked and disturbed by that. But, restudying and reanalyzing it suggests an even more fundamental issue that was posed by Edmund Burke: how can men in public life acquire imagination enough to wish to be conciliatory without being craven? Seeing how difficult, and unlikely, conciliation was in such a relatively simple situation as this one may serve to enlarge our comprehension of large scale controversies and colossal blunders like the tax on tea; imposed as it was by men, all of ability, and one of them, acute, witty, clever, imaginative and indeed brilliant: Chancellor of the Exchequer, Townshend.

Appendix A

Value Of A Case Study Of This Sort

Theory and Perspective

There is a strong emphasis in modern social science on theory. In a negative sense, of course, such a case as this contributes to theory in a formal way; for example, in disproving the oversweeping generalization of my own earlier work in Bauer, Pool, and Dexter, the case suggests a more modest statement of the values of ambiguity and fuzziness in law-making—a statement which points out the defects and dangers of fuzziness and ambiguity, also (see above, p. 4).

But, case studies seem to me valuable for a reason which does not fit into the standard notion of theory. Case studies ought, reflected upon and considered carefully, to add to people's ability to ask questions, to acquire perspectives. In this, they are similar to training in old-fashioned medical diagnosis: a fledgling physician who sees a case or cases of a certain sort knows better what questions to ask, what likenesses and differences to try to trace out between some new situation and the ones he has seen, and so on. A great deal of the value of political, sociological, and anthropological study ought, it seems to me, to lie along this line. People ought to learn to look at things better by observing and heeding cases; they ought to get a better notion of what to expect as reasonably probable, of what kinds of questions to ask, of what answers to these questions to be startled at, and what answers to regard as sensible or plausible. This is not the formal, generalized theory, at any rate which many people regard with veneration; it is a diagnostic or even a literary skill. It is also a skill of substantial importance in daily life and in the administration of large affairs where we rarely apply theory directly, but often use perspective and insight. The conscious awareness that a diagnostic skill is based upon the kinds of cases we have known and seen may help us to avoid the undue—sometimes doctrinaire—rigidity of much theory, of many canons about management, and so on.

A case study such as this one should help us look more knowledgeably (dare one say more wisely?) at other political confrontations, whether they occur among the Swat Pathans in Highland Burma, among Catholic churches in Malta, or in other Massachusetts representative town meetings. Presumably, they will provide most insight in the latter case. But one can never tell in advance whether the same interpretations apply to any new case; the insight gained from the old case provides, if you like, microscopes or telescopes which add to naked vision, and help us see more.

Appendix B

A Note On The Development Of This Study, What I Looked For, And On "Community Power" In Watertown and Belmont

This study was undertaken without any conscious attention to the much-debated issue of "community power." The field work was done before some of the best known studies had attained publication or wide circulation, of course; but stratification theory was at hand, had I thought to and chosen to use it.

As it happens, the ostensible framework within which a set of studies was undertaken, by contract with M.I.T., was to focus on the interaction of technology and local politics in the Greater Boston area. A study more concerned with technological issues than the current one was, for instance, a case study of the bitter fight about calligraphy in the schools of Brookline. (So far as I am aware, none of the other studies has been published). In fact, however, both the project director and I were charmed by the irony of a conflict in a New England town meeting in the 1950s about the locus of sovereignty: who governs by right, the people in referendum or the people in town meeting?

Although I had lived most of my life within three miles of Watertown, had driven through it innumerable times, and patronized a couple of Watertown service industries, I was in fact as unfamiliar with the way its politics operated as I was with the politics of Naples or Zurich; I knew nothing about them. I had not in my entire life known more than four people whom I could call to mind who lived in Watertown or worked there. Just as it did not occur to Watertowners to consult experts in municipal government at Harvard or Boston College because they were not in contact with such people, never ran across them, so reversely having lived on the edge of Harvard–M.I.T.–Unitarian–Belmont, a town having a limited town meeting, and as one who had worked at the State House, I knew about limited town meetings.

On the basis of my impression as to the way my own town, Belmont, had been run, I expected to find much more concentration of authority in a few hands than existed in Watertown. If I expected anything about the limited town meeting, I expected that people would be relatively indifferent or apathetic (as they certainly seemed to me generally to be in Belmont, and as they are in some other Massachusetts towns). I was startled by the degree of interest and involvement which many Watertowners showed in local politics; although in this Watertown resembles some other areas with a somewhat similar socio-economic pattern. For example, in a study my students and I did in 1957, in a local precinct preceding a special primary for a StateRepresentative in Lowell in which there were fourteen candidates, it appeared that the average voter whom we could reach for interview purposes "knew" according to his/her statement at least three of these; on the other hand, at the time of a similar special primary in Belmont, most registered Democrats interviewed by phone did not even seem to know there was such a primary or election, and many more of them were vague about what a state representative is "like" than was true in Lowell. The precincts in Belmont where interviewing took place were upper-status, upper-income, and many residents there were nationally famous; nobody in the Lowell precinct was famous at all, and the general level of status was probably a bit lower than Watertown's (more industrial workers). But, as in Watertown, most of the Lowell interviewees belonged to Lowell; some of them, apparently, had never even been to Boston (forty minutes away), and national or international issues did not impinge on their attention very much.

But until I re-read Nelson Polsby's masterly *Community Power and Political Theory*[43] in its enlarged form it did not even occur to me that in this study I had simply finessed the issue of community power as such. I was concerned with the issue at hand: how did the fight come about? I listened to what people told me, and as an interviewer,[44] tried to get them to spell out whatever seemed to them significant. I never heard any one mention any living business man of any significance. Such business men had, for the most part, moved out of Watertown; but, of course, we know of towns and cities in which influence is exercised or an attempt is made to exercise influence by those who do not live there. Nobody on either side, and no neutral, referred to or alleged that anything of the sort happened in Watertown. On the contrary, discussions about the possible influence of business firms in the Square or of the Hood in its national form suggested that people connected with these institutions for the most part did not live in Watertown and stayed out of community "squabbles." The contrast was made by a few old-timers with the way things had been or they believed they had been in the past, when there was local involvement by business figures; but that was years ago.

In some communities, even though certain classes of business men may not be active, one can expect to find realtors or lawyers engaged in real estate matters, active. This has been notably true in many Florida communities, for instance; and it would be rather surprising, although I have no data on it, if it were not true of some towns on Cape Cod. But no one was mentioned to me who was an attorney with a local practice of any significance. Since I was not thinking about community power issues as such I did not go further in my inquiries, but I rather suspect that in fact people who handled Watertown real estate as a specialty were quite different from developers in other, newer, or wealthier communities or in communities with more turn-over; I suspect indeed that a good many and probably most sales in Watertown were handled by people who did more business in Newton, Cambridge, Waltham, or Belmont. But that is an impression based on my general knowledge of the area and I did not unfortunately check it out.

Indeed, as the text shows, it is difficult to use the standard notion of different social strata in Watertown; technically, the community was too homogeneous in the 1950s. There were sharp differences between the Irish-American insiders whose families had been in the community for several generations, and the newcomer Homeowners; but these were differences of skill, perception, outlook, and of where people worked or their relatives and friends worked. If one is to regard the one group as different in "class" from the other, one would almost be adopting Granville Hicks's notion that people self-select the class to which they belong in small American communities.[45]

There were certainly cases of people who had adapted and adopted to the Watertown approach; the relatively genial acceptance of "the ADA faction" in Watertown town politics, some of whose members I believe were Jewish, and who certainly were in numerous ways sociologically different from old Watertown may be mentioned. Indeed, being "Irish" was sometimes in Massachusetts politics simply a factional matter; for some years in an adjoining Congressional district, there was competition as to whether an "Irishman," a "Jew" or occasionally a "Yankee" should be the Democratic nominee; but on several occasions the preferred "Irish" candidate, referred to as Irish, was in fact Dutch (a Dutch *Catholic*, to be sure).

Now, it is worth noting that a good many people referred, positively or negatively, to "the old Yankees", who, as pointed out, in certain ways had exercised great influence in the town. But, at least since 1900, they had been strenuously, and sometimes successfully, opposed; and the old Yankees were in any case apparently not a coherent faction on many matters of town politics anyway. There is nothing in the literature of community power which quite epitomizes the special kind of influence which, as men remembered, they could sometimes exercise. (I do not know whether what men remembered was correct; for my purposes, it was not central; and for wider purposes, what is important was not whether it was correct, but whether it could have been). An analogue in modern American society might be this: in general, on matters political, factions and interests which have a reason to do so will no doubt fight against physicians or priests, as much as against any other opposing groups. But, on some occasions, if the physicians or priests assume the cloak of professional legitimacy, on a matter where they can not be accused of individually profiting unfairly, they do have an edge; and they will confer a civic legitimacy, as a result of the feeling, where it exists, about their professional legitimacy. In somewhat the same way, the old Yankees in Watertown may have had a slight edge, because they were regarded with respect, and were identified as "knowing" the town; and on occasions of conflict regarding matters like the wages of town employees, perhaps this edge could have made a difference. The example cited in the text from a study by Alice Bauer in Cambridge wherein people opposed to fluoridation nevertheless thought that public health experts, whom they knew took the other position, should decide the matter, is in point.

This reasoning occurred to me particularly as a result of thinking about Fredrik Barth's fascinating account of the role of the Saints, descendants of Mohammed or some other great religious leader, among the Swat Pathans.[46] In many ways, they were just leaders of competing bands like other factional leaders; but on some occasions, they could exercise a power of mediation or arbitration which conferred legitimacy on an outcome. But, to really enforce such mediation or arbitration, they had to be prepared to fight recalcitrant resisters, too, although sometimes they did not have to. And, be it noted, they were called on to mediate or arbitrate on occasion; they did not necessarily just simply step in. But what elite group theory does with leadership of this sort, I do not know.

I have, of course, contrasted frequently Belmont, with its tightly-controlled politics, against Watertown's open politics. It should be pointed out that I am in the case of Belmont relying upon impression and residence; and that I never took an active part in Belmont politics myself. However, the impression I have of it was widely held among people familiar with politics in the Boston area.

It should also be pointed out that there were definite limitations on the authority of the Belmont ruling group, even if it generally did exercise control. For example, just as in Watertown and in many other Massachusetts towns, the School Committee had a different constituency than the Selectmen or town meeting members; and, although as compared with similar towns in the area, it spent its school money differently while J. Watson Flett was in command of Belmont matters; he nevertheless frequently complained about its wasteful expenditures and his inability to check them.

Furthermore, while Belmont was the home of many people of very high status, in the professions and to some extent in business, I do not know of any such person who was an active member of the organization which was supposed to run the town. For these high status people were not, as pointed out above, much interested in local affairs (except for the fact that sometimes their wives were interested in school affairs). They could not in any case spend time on them. The people who ran the town—and the Flett family—were presumably in rather direct sociological, if not genealogical, descent from the real estate developers who had first opened up the town for settlement around the time of the Civil War. But, on the whole, they would not be found in *Who's Who in America* nor did they head or represent businesses of any size; they represented only some local interests, such as concern with a low tax rate and efficient service, and a genuine concern for a "sound" community. But just as the Irish town employees in Watertown in the 1950s had not adapted to the Homeowner types, so the leadership in Belmont did not completely adapt to the change in Belmont's population after World War II. They were far more conservative than some of the new residents, especially in style. But they kept on providing good service, and most of the new residents were too preoccupied with other matters to pay much attention to town affairs; and, above all, possibly, the Belmont leadership was more astute, so it did not during this period receive any shocking challenge such as affected the Watertown town meeting.

An effective test of some of the themes which Polsby and others raise might be provided by taking a series of suburban Massachusetts towns, comparing those with comparable forms of government, and seeing who, if anybody, runs them. Impression suggests differences would be quite substantial.

Appendix C

On Equality, Inequality, And Governance In Watertown And Elsewhere

Hughes reached an interesting conclusion in his study of the Siberian Eskimo. "On the one hand," he says "yes, all men are inherently equal; but, *demonstrably,* no. Equality is supported by cultural consensus as an initial point of departure for behavior; much striving operates under this aegis and many behavioral situations are defined in this framework. But the end result of the transaction is often reaffirmation of inequality, and. . .of the authoritarian implications for future interpersonal relations derived from such ranking. Siberian Eskimo society was therefore neither egalitarian nor hierarchial*—or else it was both, if we are to type it.* (italics supplied) The label used would have to be justified by the statistical preponderance of classes of actions performed under the implicit justification of one ideological order as against another; and in this case it is difficult to infer a tendency predominant enough to warrant use of the single typological label."[47]

All this may be true of numerous societies which, ideologically, place high importance on equality. Because, in fact, desiring control, effectiveness, efficiency, and know-how, knowledge, and skill, they will on many occasions in fact propose some sort of hierarchy. This would seem to be the case in Watertown; the insiders with know-how and skill were in fact respected by many people in town and in the final analysis the town did not reject their control because it seemed reasonable. At the same time, there was a veneration for the notion of equality of all.

Hughes points out that Leach faced the same problem in describing the political behavior of the Kachin.[48] Among the Kachin, Leach found, "two apparently conflicting ideal types of political structure, one authoritarian and hierarchical (called) gumsa," the other "egalitarian (called) gumlao. . ."

If such an interpretation is correct, the questions in a society or community stressing egalitarian values are: when are they employed? how are they set aside or what contravening virtues are cherished? and so on.

Appendix D

On The Use Of The Term Sovereignty

Of course, no one in Watertown, in his right mind, believed that Watertown was or could be "sovereign" in the sense of being the final power. Every informed American, presumably, knows that on most matters the Federal, or the State, government is sovereign in this sense.

However, there is no one word of which I know that is better fitted to denote the conception of being the final power *in the locality or community*. The dictionary defines "sovereign" as also meaning "controlling influence" or as "having undisputed ascendancy." In these senses, the debate in Watertown was as to which "town meeting"–the representative town meeting or the town meeting in referendum–had ascendancy or controlling influence.

It may also be worthy of note that Bernard Crick's article on *Sovereignty* in the 1968 edition of the Encyclopedia of the Social Sciences speaks of sovereignty as a notion which applies in case of emergency. In fact, the arguments of counsel for the Town employees and of Judge Swift in his Superior Court decision were based on a contemplation of emergency, as reported above; they maintained that because salaries to police, firefighters, and so on, dealt with emergency situations, these could not properly be discussed or debated through a referendum procedure, but would have to be considered and decided in the more exacting scrutiny of a town meeting.

One important reason for the use of the term "sovereignty" here is the reminder which it gives of the similarities between the arguments of the 1770s about whether the British Parliament (which "virtually" but not directly represented the colonists) could legitimately tax them. The Watertown argument revolved around the contention that citizens could not legitimately be represented and therefore were not legitimately taxed by a body, many of whose members *were also* salaried employees of the town, which raises the question of the 1770s in a different context.

Footnotes

1. The field work and original draft of this study, 1958–59, were supported by contract with Massachusetts Institute of Technology, Department of Political Science, under a Falk Foundation grant. I am grateful. Neither MIT nor Falk are responsible for any errors of commission by the author. I am still more grateful to the Watertowners who talked with and helped me.

2. C. V. Wedgewood, *The King's Peace, 1637–41,* (New York: Macmillan, 1955), gives an excellent presentation of the situation in his reign.

3. Often reprinted, the same theme is found throughout Burke's speeches.

4. E. E. Schattschneider, *The Semi-Sovereign People: A Realist's View of Democracy in America,* (New York: Holt, Rinehart, & Winston, 1960), p. 3 and p. 29.

5. *Stratagems and Spoils* (New York: Schocken, 1969).

6. See David B. Truman, *The Governmental Process,* (New York: Knopf, 1951), a book organized around "the rules of the game."

7. Robert Luce, *Legislative Problems,* (Boston: Houghton Miflin, 1935), is still one of the first-rate discussions on the values of procedure.

8. Except possibly by T. V. Smith, *Legislative Way of Life,* (Chicago: University of Chicago Press, 1940) (recently reissued).

9. M. J. Swartz, Introduction to his *Local-Level Politics: Social and Cultural Perspectives,* (Chicago: Aldine, 1968).

10. *Ibid.*

11. See Lewis A. Dexter, *Sociology and Politics of Congress,* (Chicago: Rand McNally, 1970), Part II, for a more extensive discussion of political attention (to appear in an expanded edition, New Brunswick, N. J.: Transaction Books, probably 1982, under another title).

12. R. Bauer, I. Pool, and L. Dexter, *American Business and Public Policy,* 2nd ed. (Chicago: Aldine, 1972) p. 79.

13. Wm. A. Gamson, "Rancorous Conflict in Community Politics," *American Sociological Review*, 31 (1966): 71–81. Gamson does not include town employee wage conflicts among the issues which he considers. His study, as reported in this article, pays far less attention to the historical and political antecedents or correlates of conflict than is done in the present report.

14. See Elwyn E. Mariner, *This is Your Massachusetts Government*, 7th edn., (Arlington Hts., Mass: Mariner Books, 1973), p. 39, for a list of Massachusetts towns which abandoned the open town meeting. Two of the 45 while retaining the statutory name "town" adopted in effect a "city" form of government. (I am grateful to Mr. Mariner for this information). The other 43 adopted a limited town meeting.

It will also be noticed that about one eighth of all towns had abandoned open town meetings by 1973 (about one-third of the towns over 6,000 in population which are eligible to do so) whereas since 1921 no town become legally a city.

I consulted Mr. Mariner, Prof. J. F. Zimmerman, and others, and have not located any *general* discussion of limited town meetings or related developments.

In Connecticut, (see Patricia Stuart, *Forms of Town and City Government in Connecticut,* [Storrs, Conn., Institute of Public Service, U. Connecticut, 1970], $2.00, pp. 11–2. I am grateful to Miss Stuart for updating by letter the material in this report), there were in 1973 six towns having a representative town meeting, although they varied, apparently, considerably from the Massachusetts form.

In Rhode Island (letter from Professor Elmer Cornwell, Brown University, February 12, 1973, to whom I am grateful) "Under the home rule amendment to the state constitution towns in many cases (have) written new charters for themselves and in a fair number of these instances have abolished the town meeting in the process. In those cases, the town council becomes the legislative body of the town perhaps supplemented by some sort of finance committee or something of the kind. . .As to the matter of representative town meetings, this device has not been adopted anywhere in the state as yet. I've worked with three or four charter commissions as consultant and the question has come up. We could not decide on the basis of anything available whether there was a legal bar in the constitution or laws of the state to the adoption of such a device. . . .My personal feeling is that. . .logically, if they can take the longer step, they could also take the shorter step. . ."

Brattleboro, Vermont, has had a limited town meeting since 1961 (I am grateful to Professor Rolf Haugen and the Town Clerk of Brattleboro for information on this point). There seems to have been some discussion of such a possibility in Sanford, Maine, but apparently no town in Maine nor New Hampshire has actually adopted the limited town meeting. (The town meeting system had sporadic offshoots in areas settled from New England (see for instance Murray Beck's interesting discussion of *The Evolution of Municipal Government in Nova Scotia,* 125 pp., 1972, a report to the Royal Commission (Nova Scotia) on Education, Public Services, and Provincial-Municipal Relations, showing that on the "South Shore" of Nova Scotia, town meetings of a sort were tried for about a century against prohibitions from the provincial capitol) but has never seriously developed elsewhere, as far as I know.)

(Also, J. H. Aitchison in his doctoral dissertation on municipal government in Ontario reports the extra-legal efforts of settlers in that province (1790–93) to institute town meetings according to the New England model. "The very first bill to be introduced in the legislature of Upper Canada (Ontario) was one to authorize town meetings for the purpose of appointing various parish officers." However, the Government insisted on the appointment of officers by quarter sessions. The Government, however, after the first general elections, consented to the appointment of minor parish officers by town meetings. The conclusion of A. Shortt, quoted by Aitchison (p. 193) is that "the concession of town meetings in such a restricted form proved to be much more effective discouragement of their powers than if they had been denied altogether. . ." (from Shortt, p. 414). (J. H. Aitchison, *The Development of Local Government in Upper Canada, 1783–1850.* Unpublished Thesis, University of Toronto, 1953, pp. 186–200, quoting Adam Shortt, 'Municipal History, 1791–1876.' *In Canada and Its Provinces,* Vol. XVIII (Ontario, Part II), Edinburgh Constable 1914.) Statements are sometimes made about the "town meeting system" having been taken from New England and used in early Michigan. I have been unable to find citations which assure me that this really happened and incline to the view that occasional assemblages of citizens have been mistakenly identified as town meetings. A statement by Richard J. Hathaway (in a letter to me, August 21, 1980) seems to me correct that "no real study of the question seems to have been done. . ." and to find out would necessitate a careful analysis of the hundreds of local Michigan histories. (Hathaway is Head, Michigan Unit, State Library Service, Michigan).)

15. See League of Women Voters, *Massachusetts State Government*, 2nd ed. (Cambridge, Mass.: Harvard University Press, 1970), pp. 335–6.

16. C. Wright Mills, "Professional Ideology of Social Pathologists," in his collected essays, *Power, Politics, and People,* ed. I. L. Horowitz, (New York: Oxford University Press, 1963), pp. 525–52 (essay originally appeared in *American Journal of Sociology*, 1943).

17. Because of the greater turnover in a police department without civil service; that is, because fewer people stay in the force until the last years of relatively high pay and a pension accrual.

18. A curious parallel: cities and towns in Canada can contract on a renewal basis with the R.C.M.P. to provide local policing, or can set up their own police forces. It is believed that one reason impelling cities and towns towards the R.C.M.P. is that, since individual R.C.M.P. officers are rotated about the country, the R.C.M.P. handles pensions nationally, whereas a local police force will at some point have to pension off its own policemen.

19. See concrete discussions of this distinction in John Beattie, *The Nyoro State,* (Clarendon Press: Oxford, 1971), esp. pp. 62 ff., and in S. Nadel, *A Black Byzantium,* (London: Oxford Press, 1942), pp. 72 ff. See also the theoretical analysis of the issue in E. E. Evans-Pritchard, *Social Anthropology and other essays,* New York: Free Press, 1962), "Anthropology and History," pp. 172–92.

20. For example, in Belmont (and adjoining Arlington) in 1931 there were a large number of Wellington households—see the phone book for the Wellington name—and there were many other households related to the Wellingtons. Roger Wellington originally settled what is now Belmont in 1696. But by 1973 the number of Wellingtons in the Western suburban book had become a fraction of what it was in 1932; and in order to get any information about some Wellingtons who built some historic Belmont houses, Belmont historians had to write to California.

Similarly, in Shelburne, Nova Scotia—a Yankee town, practically entirely, although in Nova Scotia—a Dexter who flourished in the early part of the 19th century has at least seventy-five mature descendents and so did a Bruce of the same period. Only two of these people under the age sixty-five lived in Shelburne by 1964, and only five others lived anywhere in New England or Nova Scotia; the rest were scattered over Canada and the United States. The two living in Shelburne, typically, had less formal education than at least half the others.

21. For the outstanding treatment of the taking over of locally owned firms by national ones, written from a New England perspective, that of Newburyport, Massachusetts, see W. L. Warner and J. O. Low, *The Social System of the Modern Factory* (New Haven: Yale University Press, 1947).

22. The year after I conducted this study in Watertown (1959) was the year in which a number of businessmen made a great fashion (rhetorically) out of participation in politics. I conducted a series of interviews, under the supervision of Oliver Garceau, then Visiting Professor at Harvard, with business leaders about their firm's encouragement (or discouragement) of political participation. At that time, and for several years thereafter, it appeared that in fact, although some business firms would encourage middle management to take part in politics (and after all, Watertown plants and retail stores were run by people of middle management status) no national headquarters appeared to have confronted the obvious problem: suppose some middle management person takes this rhetoric seriously, and gets criticized and perhaps makes trouble for the firm, because he takes a stand on some local issue, of no particular concern to the firm? What happens?

Or, in 1953 to 1955, as part of the study which led to R. Bauer, I. Pool, and L. Dexter, *American Business and Public Policy* (New York: Atherton, 1963; 2nd edn., 1972) we constantly ran across reaction to the stand on reciprocal trade (in favor) taken by no less a person than Henry Ford II. At that time, expanded foreign trade was of great value to automobile makers. Nevertheless, throughout the country Ford dealers and representatives, and Detroit management (because of the negative reaction of Ford dealers and representatives to Henry Ford's position) emphasized that Mr. Ford spoke only for himself. This was not a company position. The reason was very simple: in glass-manufacturing communities, for instance, and in coal areas (glass and coal being at that time quite afraid of increased foreign imports) there was considerable talk of boycotting Ford cars because of Mr. Ford's position. Yet, Ford, unlike local managers in Watertown, controlled the company.

23. F. G. Bailey, ed., *Gifts and Poison: The Politics of Reputation,* (New York: Schoken Books, 1971).

24. Analogically, it is to be expected that student protests in 1969 to 1970 hurt faculty worst in those colleges where faculty had felt themselves honored and respected most. Since faculty contacts are chiefly with a minority of students, faculty might be very wrong about the likelihood of protest.

It would have been, of course, desirable to study other communities comparatively. In many ways, this sketch of the Watertown conflict could be regarded as an agenda for studying local political conflicts in any region comparatively. Unfortunately, the study was budgeted at $1,000—and most of what I am now proposing did not occur to me until 1973, some of it not until 1980; I mulled over the analysis for a long time, returning to it actively on several occasions.

25. As showing how public foci of attention make a difference: (1) although myself brought up as and by conviction a strong feminist, I simply did not notice the "male, chauvinist" nature of this argument in 1957, nor until 1973, (2) and nor did representatives of librarians, etc., make a protest about it at the time, as far as I know. Things would have been different in 1979.

26. Some people thought it relevant that at the time the town officers were mostly Republican, whereas police and fire were believed to lean Democratic.

27. The queasiness at the time of enactment about the original statute was very great, so far as I have been able to reconstruct the 1919 situation; a good many people felt as unhappy about changing the town meeting as more recently some national legislators felt about civil rights. I assume the ambiguity in the term "town meeting" was not mere slovenliness in draftsmanship but an attempt to paper over the seriousness of the shift; at the same time, proponents of the representative town meeting made much of the referendum as preserving the essential town meeting, and of two related points: (1) the limited town meeting would be extremely large (later, after our period, Watertown did reduce its elected membership from 270 to 165—but that was in the 1960s), (2) anyone could speak, even though not anyone could vote, at town meetings. The great majority of voters do not now speak (and never did speak) at general, unlimited, town meetings either. Preservation of the right can be argued for; but if many people exercised it, town meetings, limited or unlimited, would long ago have become impossible.

28. *Op. cit.*

29. For example, a discussion could have shown how salaries compared with adjoining communities; presented the pattern of raises in other, similar communities; and argued the relevance of the question of "danger pay" (how many Watertown policemen and firemen had undergone in the past serious injuries, or better, how many do in similar communities; and how much were these risks taken account of in injury insurance, pensions,

and so on, and in the right of policemen to retire younger than most town employees?). I found myself impatient with much of the rhetoric as I encountered the issues in 1958 in that I never heard specifics advanced on any of these points.

Impressionistically, in terms of relative, real wages, many town employees seem to me (even despite the cost of living bonus) to have been getting less in 1956, after the raises, than in 1937; but neither side really tackled that issue. Of course many other variables, like the absolute increase in proportion of town employees, greater amount of money spent on schools, etc., entered in.

30. There was relatively little discussion at any time—none on the side of the opponents of the pay raises—as to the essential economic question: Were the increased expenditures providing people with services which they wanted and needed? at a reasonable cost? During the 1950s, I myself had contact with two agencies in Watertown: the library and the recreation department. Comparatively, the latter was head and shoulders over those of Arlington, Belmont, or Cambridge (part of this no doubt due to additional recreation posts added in 1956) and Watertown did give some of its citizens more incentives to fitness and fun. The library had more accessible and usable resources than Arlington or Belmont—at that time—although the question might have been raised whether their use was great enough to justify supplying them, since Watertown is after all close to great library centers such as Boston. And, in private conversation, even some of the opponents of the town employees boasted about how the Fire Department had taken the lead in developing resuscitation services for people with heart attacks, etc.; but no one to my knowledge evaluated this activity in comparison with alternate ways of achieving the same objectives, on a cost-benefit basis.

Another point in relationship to Robinson's argument and that of the Homeowners: of course, the increase in expenditures due to actions by the state and its agencies which did happen in the particular years in question was not necessarily continuous. Indeed, as Lyman H. Ziegler had kindly pointed out to me: (letter of September 11, 1980) "You should remember that in the longer view since World War II, state aid to local government has risen spectacularly. Thus in tax rate terms there have been offsets to the rising mandated costs" (not chiefly those of the sort reported in the text but in most years such items as state-mandated pensions, state-mandated expenditures for handicapped children, and so on) "which the towns have strongly protested. . .By comparing Watertown's increase in receipts from the state. . .with the increase in state-mandated costs (between any year and any other given year, constituting a period) you may find they wash out—which would mean that the rising taxes were the town's responsibility." This could well be the case in general; but no such sophisticated argument was made by the Homeowners nor so far as I know by any one at the time of the dispute (although of course if it had occurred to the better-informed side, the town employees, it would not have been to their advantage to publicize it). But in any event the particular marked rise in taxes in the particular years in question which provoked the outburst of Homeowner activity was due to the actions of the state and its agencies (including the county).

(In terms of Zeigler's point, it is only fair to suggest the possibility that Miles Robinson, whose report on town finances is commented on adversely above, may have recognized the development of which Zeigler speaks; and so, at bottom, there may have been more to Robinson's argument than appears in his report. But, if so, neither he nor any one else involved in the controversy clarified the issues in Zeigler's terms).

A fundamental issue in Robinson's analysis may have been the choice of a base year (see Thomas Sowell, *Knowledge and Decisions,* [New York: Basic Books, 1980], pp. 136). A different base year might produce very different results.

31. The school autonomy law, GL c 71. s. 34, provided that an action may be brought against the town by ten taxable inhabitants (presumably parents or others with concern for the school) or the attorney general of Massachusetts, if the school's budgetary requests are not met by the town. Proposition 2½ approved at the general election of 1980 may lead to the end of school autonomy.

32. It is an interesting illustration of the way the position of the observer affects emphasis: in 1958, aged forty-two, this retirement base issue had no particular impact upon me, was not memorable. In 1980, aged sixty-five, and being now myself under the Massachusetts Retirement system, it seems the important substantive issue!

33. This chart was prepared by one of Robert Wood's assistants in the Falk Foundation project. His assistants also condensed considerably my original narrative account, and many sentences herein are products of their editing. I am grateful.

34. This listing shows the page on which the story appeared. Presumably a good many people saw the page 1 story at least who knew almost

nothing else about town affairs, (commuters who resided in but did not "belong to" Watertown).

35. Representative salaries under the 1955 arrangement were:

Junior Clerk Stenographer starting at $2490, going up in the fourth year to $2890

Senior Clerk Stenographer	$2890 to $3300
Purchasing Agent for the Town	$5100 to $6530
Reference Librarian	$3480 to $4280
Health Officer	$5110 to $6530
Fire Lieutenant	$4320 to $5110
Police and Fire Chiefs	$5640 to $6890

36. Of course, if a particular School Committee subsumes in its department, general library, or recreation activities which are not normally regarded as part of the schooling process, then questions arise as to precisely where the town meeting has a right to intervene.

37. See Lewis A. Dexter, "Organizational and Political Climate," *Political Methodology;* 3(1976)141–58.

38. On another occasion, several years later, when a town refused to appropriate funds which the State authorities believed it should have for health purposes, the State simply stepped in to administer the relevant local agencies, so that the children of the town, for instance, and others with whose welfare the State was concerned as "the protector of the people" should not be endangered. Although I had no personal contact at all with the matter, newspaper reports made it fairly clear that the issues involved were issues of judgement about what health programs should be adopted and carried out—it was not that the town could not have raised sufficient funds for the purposes.

39. To be sure, policemen probably have a strong stake in avoiding genuine town meeting democracy, and can only do their job well where they are buffered from direct popular control (e.g. by strong standing committees or strong selectmen). Most Massachusetts towns probably have had such strong selectmen or strong standing committees; which is to say that in fact town meeting democracy, of the mythical sort, without hierarchy, does not work in some areas of public safety. Judge Swift in fact said this, but of course he did not say so in so many words. An alternative development of his position might have been that if a town is large enough to resort to a limited town meeting it is likely to be subject to mob sentiment; and possibly, (considering some of his other opinions) he might have been sympathetic with such an argument.

One knowledgeable supporter of the position advanced by Attorney McLaughlin presented above argued: "A single policeman who is raiding gambling joints can produce enough ill-will so a lot of people will gang up in town meeting to cut all police salaries." He could have added equal ill-will may be produced by a perfectly defensible failure to respond to an emergency quickly enough for public opinion. He went ahead, "In a town like Watertown, a referendum vote is the only chance a lot of people have to take it out on the police who've stooped them for speeding. . . Whenever you submit a police matter—and there are statistics to show it for Massachusetts—seven out of ten times the police get forced down by the voters." He then went ahead to tell about a tourist community in the Berkshires where local people got so annoyed with the police for enforcing laws against illegal amusements that they, practically speaking, hamstrung the police completely, so the State Troopers informally took over the policing of the community.

40. Note: In 1965, subsequent to the period here described, the 70th Amendment to the Massachusetts Constitution was adopted, and under it an implementing Home Rule Practices Act; these are described as giving greater autonomy to towns and cities than had formerly been the case. They also provided a standard form of representative town meeting which, if adopted, would avoid the ambiguities provided by the use of the term "town meeting" in the original Watertown Act. See League of Women Voters, op. cit., pp. 343f.

41. One reason, perhaps, why town officials and employees did not consult Harvard, one of the more natural places to check with, may be found in a poem by Leonard Bacon which I have not located but remember reading forty-five years ago about "the young man from Watertown" who travelled every day to Harvard on the street car, where he did not "speak to anyone" and "was spoken to by nobody." After four years he went up on the platform, at commencement, was handed his diploma, "speaking to no one and spoken to by nobody," and then got back onto the street car and went back to Watertown. This may explain Harvard; but of course it does not quite explain the University of Massachusetts or Boston College.

42. See F. Bird and F. Ryan, *The Recall of Public Officers in California* (New York: Macmillan, 1930), p. 117. The general theme of the universality of politics is best stated in J.D.B. Miller, *The Nature of Politics* (Harmondsworth, England: Penguin), 1962.

The Bird and Ryan reports are fascinating to the political buff. But although they assert the universality of politics at all levels, the fact that its phenomena are common, they do not at all demonstrate that point case by individual case, phenomenon by phenomenon. An effort to do so might make their stories less fascinating; but it would probably have represented more of a contribution to awareness had they tried to show the general meaning of each case.

43. Nelson Polsby, *Community Power and Political Theory,* Second Edition (New Haven: Yale Univ. Press, 1980).

44. See my *Elite and Specialized Interviewing,* (Evanston, Ill.: Northwestern Univ. Press, 1970), for a discussion of my method of collecting data, with a few specific comments on the Watertown study.

45. Granville Hicks *Small Town* (New York: Macmillan, 1946). (I wrote this note on *Small Town* from recollection and on checking the text do not find that Hicks actually makės such a statement therein. But I do have a clear impression of either reading or hearing Hicks make such an interpretation of his work, and it conforms, it seems to me, quite clearly to his report on his small town).

46. Fredrik Barth, *Political Leadership Among Swat Pathans,* (London: Athlone Press, 1964). See Fred Bailey's use of the Pathan Saints in his *Stratagems and Spoils* (New York: Schocken, 1969), p. 64.

47. Charles C. Hughes, "Structure, Field and Process in Siberian Eskimo Political Behavior" pp. 163-89 of M. J. Swartz (ed.), *op. cit.,* reference footnote 9, quotation from p. 170.

48. Edmund Leach, *Political Systems of Highland Burma* (Boston: Beacon Press, 1954).